NEVER TRY TO NEGOTIATE WITH A DRUNKEN HOMEOWNER

...and 800 Other Things Every Real Estate Agent Should Know

———— ◆ ————

Matt Williams

Matt Williams

© **Matt Williams, 2017**

Acknowledgement

I may be the one who put the words on paper, but this book was co-authored by hundreds of real estate professionals who in some form found their way into my life. There is no way to acknowledge them all, but I would like to offer a word of thanks to those trainers, mentors, authors, managers and agents who have been part of my journey and have taught me everything I know.

Thanks also to Sarah Williams and my sister Cindy for their contributions to the cover design, and to Liz Comperiati for her enthusiastic support of all I have tried to do for the last 15 years.

And to Beverly, without whom none of this would have been possible.

Matt Williams

Disclaimer

Real estate transactions and the real estate sales business often involve complex legal issues. Laws vary by state and a practice acceptable in one jurisdiction may not be legal in another. Nothing in this book is intended to be contrary to the law or the Realtor® Code of Ethics. It is recommended that you check with your attorney before implementing any policy or practice that is contained in this book.

———◆———

A word about gender

My use of the pronouns 'his' or 'her' throughout this book is entirely random and arbitrary. No prejudice is intended and none should be inferred by the use of either gender with respect to any issue covered in this book.

Matt Williams

Everything happens to everybody sooner or later if there is time enough.

\-   George Bernard Shaw

Matt Williams

Contents

Section 3 – Your Office

Section 4 – Getting Listings

Section 5 – Servicing The Listing

Section 6 – Open Houses

Section 7 – Working With Buyers

Section 8 – Learning Along The Way

Introduction

To most people, the job of a real estate agent doesn't seem very complex or difficult. I know that was my thinking 30 years ago when my wife and I bought our first home. Our agent showed us a few houses, we picked one we liked, made an offer, and a few weeks later we closed. The whole process looked pretty simple and the fact the agent made an easy $1,000 was one of the reasons I decided to leave my job with an air cargo company in favor of a career in real estate sales.

Three decades later I can say with confidence that my initial assessment of the real estate sales business was wrong. It is neither simple nor easy. Actually, it didn't take me 30 years to learn this. I realized it within months of getting my license when I listed the home of Gunnar Ryan.

Gunnar was basically a good guy when he was sober but abusive when he drank. The trouble for me was he drank nearly every night. He'd start in with the gin around 6 PM and then call me around 8. He'd yell, curse, and threaten to fire me. Then he'd hang up. The next day his wife would call to apologize.

I don't recall there being a chapter in license school on how to deal with people like Gunnar. In fact, there are hundreds of situations (like dealing with a drunken homeowner) that real estate agents face all the time. The problems come fast and from all directions so that sometimes it feels like we are playing tennis against five opponents. As I experienced firsthand more of the challenges real estate agents must deal with, it made me truly appreciate good agents.

A good real estate agent is a marvel. She shifts from one negotiation to another as fast as she can end one phone call to take the next. At 10 o'clock she is at a closing and then at noon she is ankle-deep in water looking for the water main shut off at her vacant house listing. After calling the plumber she peels off her boots, puts her shoes back on and heads out to show her buyer client four houses at 1:30. She'll grab a hurried dinner at a fast food drive-thru while listening through her Bluetooth headset to one of her seller clients complain, "Why should I have to clean my house for showings? Buyers should be able to look past the mess" and "Why haven't you shown my house".

At 7:00 P.M. she has a listing appointment where she spends much of her time explaining to the sellers what they paid for the house ten years ago has nothing to do with what it is worth today. She gets home, exhausted, at 9:30. Before she can relax however she has 2 phone messages to return and 4 emails she must answer. Tomorrow she will do it all again with a different cast of demanding clients and a new set of problems – none of which she created, all of which she is expected to fix.

Real estate sales as a career can be lucrative, rewarding, fun, and a great way to make a living. But it can also be frustrating, infuriating, depressing, and a road to poverty.

From the very beginning of my real estate career, I have been fascinated why some agents succeed while other agents fail. That fascination has led me on a quest for answers that has involved reading hundreds of books, attending dozens of seminars, studying the teachings of great coaches, and observing the everyday practices – good and bad - of hundreds of real estate agents.

I have learned that the essence of success in real estate sales is found in what agents do. Top producing agents do the right things more consistently than agents who fail. It is as simple as that.

So what are 'the right things'? For years I have recorded many notes and observations of things I have seen agents do right, as well as things I've seen agents do wrong. This book is the sum of those observations. It is in no way a complete distillation of the real estate sales business, but it does account for those things that made enough of an impression on me to write them down.

Understanding how busy real estate agents are, I wanted to put this information in a convenient, easy-to-access format. I wanted a resource anyone could use even if they only had a couple minutes while waiting for a customer to show up or in between visitors at an open house. Presenting the information in lists seemed like the best idea.

My hope is that you learn many things from my experiences. However, if you find (or rediscover) even one idea or one concept that contributes to you being a better agent for your clients and a more successful professional, then my purpose in writing this book will have been fulfilled.

I wish you the best.

Matt Williams

Section 1

———•———

A Career in
Real Estate Sales

Matt Williams

14 Characteristics Of Great Real Estate Agents

Each may do his or her business in different ways, but there are certain traits common to all top producing agents. Here's a list.

1. **They are resilient** – This business comes with disappointment. Sometimes that disappointment can be crushing. Top agents know how to brush themselves off and get back in the game.

2. **They are persistent** - Many sales are made after the prospect says 'no'. And then says 'no' again. Top producers understand this and do not accept the first (or second or third) 'no' as the final word.

3. **They are hard working** – There is no other way around it, top producers work hard. Thomas Edison said genius was 1% inspiration and 99% perspiration. He was right.

4. **They are focused** – Top producers have their sights set on their objectives and work towards them nearly all the time.

5. **They accept responsibility for their success** – They know their success or failure is entirely up to them. They would not want it any other way.

6. **They are responsive** – Top producers understand that time kills all opportunities. There is nothing to be gained by waiting until tomorrow to call that prospect – they do it now.

7. **They invest in their business** – Successful agents understand money spent wisely is an investment. They also know while they are not investing, their competition is and taking business from them.

8. **They believe in themselves** – Top producing agents want to be in control of their business. They want to make the decisions on matters that affect them.

9. **They are opportunistic** – High producers leave no opportunity, however small, unexplored.

10. **They look ahead** – They are students of the business looking ahead to the next great prospecting tool, management tool, market conditions, or anything that may affect their business. They do not like surprises and they hate being left behind.

11. **They are not complacent** – Rare is the top producer who reaches the point where she says "that's enough". Like a football player who wins the Super Bowl ring and then sets out to win another and another, top producing agents are always looking ahead to the next challenge.

12. **They are acutely aware what is going on with their business** – Top producers know how much they spend to generate leads and what kind of return they get. They work from a plan, make adjustments to the plan, and generally are in tune with every aspect of their business.

13. **They are good communicators** – It's not enough to have the answers, you need to be able to convey those answers to clients and customers in a way they understand.

14. **They are patient** – Not everything happens at the pace we may want. Great agents understand this and wisely accept that some decisions, actions, and events take time.

Key Takeaway

Every single characteristic listed here is the result of choice. Top real estate agents are not great because they are born a certain way. They are top agents because they choose to be.

13 Things That Affect An Agent's Income That They Control Completely

As a real estate agent, your income is influenced by many factors, some outside of your control. Employment, interest rates, consumer confidence, and the general business climate – all are beyond your influence. That's why it is important that you control the things you can to the best of your ability. Here are 13 things that influence your income that you have 100% control over.

1. **Your attitude** - How you choose to view the events around you is your choice.

2. **Your preparedness** – If you're caught unprepared you have no one to blame but yourself.

3. **The way you present yourself** – How you dress, the way you stand, the words you use – all are within your control.

4. **Your punctuality** – Whether you're on time or not is entirely up to you. Build in a buffer to account for unforeseen difficulties that may cause you to be late.

5. **How you spend your time** – Responsibilities may at times obligate you, but for most people, the overwhelming majority of what they do with their 24 hours each day is within their control.

6. **How you react to events** - You may not be able to control what happens to you, but you have total control over how you react to what happens to you.

7. **What you eat** – Your body is a machine and a machine needs fuel. The right fuel makes your machine run better while the wrong fuel makes your machine run worse. You are

the one that chooses what type of fuel you allow into your body.

8. **How much rest you get** – Stay up late to watch a forgettable TV show or go to bed so you are properly rested for tomorrow's challenges? It's your choice.

9. **What influences you expose yourself to** – The things we read, view, and listen to (newspapers, TV, radio, etc.) all are within your control. Expose yourself to a steady diet of positive influences and you will be a positive person. Expose yourself to negative influences and you will be negative person. You choose.

10. **The people you associate with** – Whom you surround yourself with plays a major role in your success (or lack thereof). It has been said if you want to estimate your income, take the average income of the three people you spend the most time with.

11. **Your commitment to personal excellence** – Do you care about doing well or is good enough good enough? You and you alone make that choice.

12. **How you treat others** – Patience, understanding, compassion – are all within our control. So are rudeness, sarcasm, and impatience. We are the ones who decide.

13. **How you let the past affect you** – Everyone has issues from the past - damaged relationships, disappointments, or failures just to name a few. You can't change them but you can keep them from affecting your future. It may not be easy, but it is your choice.

5 Reasons New Agents Fail

The numbers are sobering. The majority of new real estate agents fail to last in the business long enough to renew their license. Here are five reasons new agents fail to make the grade.

1. **They simply don't belong in the business in the first place** - The barrier to entry in real estate sales is low. Take a course, pass a test, get a broker to sponsor you and you are a real estate agent. But are you really? Holding a real estate license and being a productive real estate agent are two different things. Many agents simply don't possess the skill sets or psychological makeup necessary to be a real estate agent. They don't particularly like people, they want to work regular 9 to 5 hours, commission sales makes them anxious, etc. A lot fewer people would wash out of the business in their first year if they knew what it really meant to be a real estate agent.

2. **They don't understand what the business is about** - Many new agents get their real estate license right after buying a house. They concluded that it didn't look too hard so they could make it in the business. They see fun times looking at houses, laughs at the closing table, and the agent walking away with a fat check. Who wouldn't want to do this? The problem is, they don't see the disappointment, the long hours, inconsistent income, and all the other things that make this business such a challenge. They don't understand that this is a business of prospecting for new clients and inherent in that is rejection – a lot of rejection.

3. **They don't have the support of the family** - There are many agents whose husbands love the idea of their wife bringing home an extra $40,000 a year…until it means that dinner may not be on the table every day at 6:00 PM, the weekend may not be free, the new real estate agent may be grouchy and/or distracted from time to time, and there may be a need to invest money not yet earned in order to grow the

new business. Having the support of those who depend on you is critical to success in real estate sales, especially in the beginning (see List #9).

4. **They join the wrong real estate company** - New agents need training, support, and a capable manager who cares about their success. Many agents join the company closest to their home regardless of whether there is training or a mentoring program. New agents only have a six-month window (at most) to get their career on track. If they join the wrong company and don't realize it in time, they may have doomed their career before it ever has a chance to get started.

5. **They simply don't work hard enough** - When a new agent starts with the idea that this business is easy, they become shocked when they realize there is hard work in being a real estate agent. It's not like digging ditches but it is difficult. It's a different kind of challenge. Calling strangers, attending training sessions, getting home at 10 o'clock at night - all are not easy and unfamiliar to many agents prior to them becoming agents. If most agents would just work – doing the things successful agents do - they would see a marked increase in their income and fewer would fail.

7 Reasons Experienced Agents Fail

There are many that believe if you can survive the first two years of your real estate career you can survive 20 years. This is largely true. What you learn the first two years can set you on the path to success . . but not always. Experienced agents do sometimes fail and leave the business. Here are 7 reasons why.

1. They stopped doing the things that made them successful – As a new agent they did all the things they were taught to do. They came to the office early, called FSBOs, had their car, briefcase, and desk organized, attended office meetings, etc. As their business grew, the demands on their time meant some things had to go. Ironically, often these were the very things that created the business that caused the time crunch.

2. They got lazy - They used to wear a jacket and tie to the office, do an hour of research before showing houses, and think carefully before writing an ad. Now they go to the office in whatever clothes they may have on, know nothing about the houses they are showing, and write banal ads during commercials while watching TV.

3. They didn't have an outlet for the frustration of this business and it manifests itself in bitterness – Bright-eyed and enthusiastic is how most agents begin their careers, but years of disappointment and frustration can sour an agent's outlook towards life in general and the real estate sales business in particular. This isn't good. You need to find a way to be that bright-eyed hopeful agent even after years of dealing with all our business throws at us.

4. They didn't work from an effective business plan – They decide they know all there is to know and rather than make things happen, they let things happen. If you are not directing your business, eventually it is not likely it will be what you want it to be.

5. **They got caught up in too many distractions** – Whether it is admirable distractions (charity, community involvement), or not so admirable distractions (office politics and rumor, golf clubs in the trunk, etc.), anything that takes your focus away from your work during working hours is going to be a drag on your business. We all have distractions. How you deal with these distractions plays a big part in the health of your business.

6. **They failed to keep up with the business** – Rather than learning about and investing in new systems and technologies, they don't grow and do business the same way they always have. Spencer Johnson's terrific book, "Who Moved My Cheese" teaches it is not a matter of 'if' the cheese will move, but 'when' it will move. If you think you can do business as you always have, you are destined to declining production and maybe even extinction.

7. **They stopped investing in prospecting** – Once their business begins to seemingly chug along on its own, many agents decide that they no longer need to 'prime the pump' by investing in prospecting. Big mistake. As Jim Collins points out in his book 'Good to Great', the seeds of failure are sewn in good times. Even when things are going well, smart agents continue to invest in prospecting.

Key Takeaway

In nearly every instance where an agent experiences a decline in her business it is directly attributable to her action (or inaction). In other words, she is the cause of her decline. The good news is the opposite is also true. Agents who succeed do so because of what they do. The great news is the choice is entirely up to you.

10 Ways To Grow Your Business When You Are Already Doing Well

In his best-selling book, 'Good To Great', author Jim Collins argues that the seeds of failure are sown in good times. When things are going well we tend to think they always will. But that's a recipe for disaster. <u>Especially</u> when things are going well you need to be looking ahead to ways to grow your business. No business stands still – it is either growing or shrinking. Here are 10 things an agent can do to grow her business when things are already going well.

1. Seek out the company of agents doing more business than you do - When you associate with higher producing agents your production rises. The example your colleagues set has a great impact on your own business. Associate with disciplined, professional, productive agents and you will become more disciplined, professional, and productive.

2. Set specific, meaningful, and challenging goals – When things are going well, it is easy to become complacent. Maybe you don't return phone calls as quickly as you used to. Maybe you skip doing a few open houses or sending out your 'Just Sold' postcards. If you set your sights on your goals (your future) and not current successes (your present) you are unlikely to fall into the trap of bad habits.

3. Update your listing literature – You can probably list houses with your eyes closed and one hand tied behind your back. That's not the point. By examining your pre-listing package and your listing presentation you likely will find places for improvement. Your visuals may be outdated, you may not have information on a new service you provide, and the general presentation may be 'tired'. Keep your message fresh.

4. Mentor a new agent – If there is a talented, motivated new agent in your company, offer to mentor him. Spending time with an eager beaver may inspire you. And there are few better ways to get better at something than to teach others how to do it.

5. Double your investment in lead generation – Generally agents spend far too little on lead generation. You are making money now, don't be cheap. Invest a significant portion of your newfound wealth into ensuring that this good fortune will continue.

6. Start building a team – Your investment in lead generation will provide you with opportunities. You don't want to lose a single one. Take that new agent (from #4 above) whom you agreed to mentor and start feeding him with leads that you don't have time to service. Besides empowering the new agent, you will have developed an additional stream of revenue with the referral income these otherwise lost opportunities will generate. It is a win-win.

7. Add a prospecting system – Over time, many agents tend to drop activities and systems that either bore them or otherwise leave them unsatisfied. Eventually they end up utilizing only prospecting systems that are familiar and comfortable. Big mistake. Read, "Who Moved My Cheese" by Dr. Spencer Johnson. Your systems may be adequate now but it is certain that some day they will not. The time to fix the roof is when the sun is shining. Always be looking for new and more effective systems. It's certain your competition is.

8. Go back to your habits from your early days in real estate – If you are fortunate enough to have saved your appointment books from the early part of your career, go back and read them. You will likely be amazed. You hustled because you had to. Revisit your early days and take a lesson from the younger (and hungrier) you.

9. Ask someone to hold you accountable – The very act of confessing your need for accountability demonstrates a healthy awareness of the human tendency to coast. A familiar law of physics is that an object at rest remains at rest and an object in motion remains in motion, unless acted upon by an outside force. An accountability partner may be just the force to keep you in motion.

10. Volunteer in your community – Giving back your time and money to others is a decent thing to do. Who knows – someday you might need someone's help. But when we volunteer we also expand our sphere of influence. When we serve on library boards, or deliver meals to elderly, or serve on a committee, we are getting the opportunity to develop deeper relationships with others. That's always good.

Matt Williams

7 Specific Actions That Will Help Jumpstart A Stalled Business

If you find your business stalled and you're not sure what to do to get it going again, a good practice is to focus on specific activities you can do today that will get your business rolling again. You can even make a game of it, assigning points for various activities. Each day you can try to better your score from the day before. Here are 7 things you can start doing and measuring today.

1. **Hand out business cards** – Make a point of putting 5 business cards in your pocket and don't go home until you have given all 5 out.

2. **Mail to potential sellers and/or buyers** – Every great agent uses direct mail to initiate new relationships. They do so because it works. The key is consistency and volume.

3. **Talk to people face to face**– My favorite trainer, Floyd Wickman, is fond of saying, "When the going gets tough, the tough get back to the basics. And the most basic thing we do is talk to people." The #1 action an agent can employ to jumpstart his business is simply talk to more people. Knock on doors, attend networking workshops, drop in on a former client – talk to people.

4. **Call people on the phone**– See # 3.

5. **Show (more) houses** – Some buyers want you to show them just one or two houses that they have selected. Pick one more house they didn't ask to see (but you think meets their needs) and show it to them. Sometimes one of these extra houses will be just what the buyer wants.

6. **Host open houses** – We'll talk more about open houses later in this book, but anything you do that puts you in front of buyers and sellers is good. See # 3.

7. **Send emails** – If you are sending emails because you are afraid to talk to people this isn't going to help much and you should probably look for another line of work. But if you are doing everything else and email is being used to supplement the more effective means to reaching out to people, the more emails you send the more opportunities you will have.

Key Takeaway

Real estate is a business of 'doing'. The best thing you can 'do' to make your business active is talk to people, especially those interested in buying or selling real estate.

17 Things Clients Say They Want From Their Real Estate Agent

One of the great joys of my work is reading letters of praise for my agents. Looking beyond the complement to my company, the words of these appreciative clients serve as a guide for what they consider important in a real estate agent. Here, taken from actual letters and emails, are what clients say is important to them.

1. "You really <u>cared</u> about our situation."

2. "Your <u>positive attitude</u> helped lift us up."

3. You were very <u>patient</u> with us.

4. "You were <u>relentless</u> in your follow-up on our behalf."

5. "You <u>had our best interest</u> at heart."

6. "We respect your <u>professionalism.</u>"

7. "You <u>left no stone unturned</u> in helping us find our home."

8. "You are <u>efficient</u> and <u>thorough.</u>"

9. "She <u>listened</u> well."

10. "Her unending <u>focus was on what would be best for us.</u>"

11. "Her <u>friendliness</u> made it an enjoyable experience."

12. "She <u>kept us informed</u> every step of the way."

13. "You were very <u>respectful.</u>"

14. "You <u>offered sound ideas.</u>"

15. "He <u>never made us feel like we were a nuisance.</u>"

16. "<u>When she said she would do something, she did it.</u>"

17. "She <u>went the extra mile</u> for us."

8 Things Agents Do That Upset Clients

When you consider that buyers and sellers of real estate are going through a very stressful time, it's not surprising that they may be hyper-sensitive and emotional. Things they could brush off under normal circumstances aren't as easily tolerated when they are under pressure. Still, it would be wrong to attribute every complaint against an agent to stress. Sometimes agents do things that they shouldn't do. Here are 8 common complaints of buyers and sellers:

1. **"She doesn't return phone calls."** – Make a commitment to return all calls within 1 hour. Then do it. You will score big points with your clients.

2. **"He was very rushed with me."** – Nothing says "You are an annoyance to me" more than making a client feel you are already thinking of what you need to do next when you are still with them.

3. **"He made me feel like I am not important to him."** – I once worked for a broker who always said, "People don't care what you know until they know that you care." He was right.

4. **"He only cares about making a commission."** – There's no quicker way to lose the support and confidence of a client than to make them feel as if they are only a commission to you.

5. **"She never gives us feedback after showings."** – Tracking down agents who showed your listing for feedback is a hassle but their comments may reinforce what you have been telling the seller about price and/or condition.

6. **"I <u>only hear from her</u> when she wants to lower the price."** – You should be communicating with your clients at least once a week. See List # 48.

7. **"He <u>does not do what he says</u> he will do."** – Make it a practice to under promise and over deliver, not the other way around.

8. **"I <u>don't think she listens</u> to what I say."** – A good practice is to repeat back what you have been told to ensure that a) you understand, and b) your client knows she has been heard.

Key Takeaway

The reason many clients turn on agents is they feel unimportant to the agent. You can prevent your clients becoming upset with you by communicating regularly, being genuinely interested in their needs, and demonstrating professionalism by doing what you say you will do.

8 Ways to Get Your Family On Board With Your Real Estate Career

It is not easy being the spouse or child of a real estate agent. Phone calls interrupt family time, the inconsistency of income sometimes makes for a tense household, dinners are often eaten cold, and fun times are sometimes scuttled when an out-of-town buyer shows up and has just one day to buy a house. Without the support of family, your business will never be as successful as it could be. Here are 8 things you can do to get the support of your family.

1. **Appreciate that it is not easy being the spouse or child of a real estate agent** – It's not easy being you but it's not easy being them either. Being aware of that will help you be more patient with them.

2. **Incorporate your loved one's goals into your goals** – The kids will accept the occasional interruption to your family time better if they see it is part of a greater good. As you develop your goals, be sure to include things they want (trip to Disney, a pool, etc.).

3. **Share your goals with your family and tell them why they are important to you** – Let everyone know why you work, what the measure of success is, and why this matters to you (and by extension, them).

4. **Share your schedule with your family and stick to it** – The occasional last minute interruptions are inevitable but what really frustrates (and angers) family is when they are made to feel your work is more important than they are. One way to show that is not the case is to post your schedule on the refrigerator with ample 'family time' blocked out in ink.

5. Celebrate successes – new listings, closed sales – as a family – It doesn't have to be expensive – a pizza or trip to the ice cream stand is fine. What you are looking to do is tie your work (and success) to something pleasing to them. Soon they'll be asking 'So when are you going to have another closing?'

6. Be sure to have a private outlet to deal with the disappointment that is part of this business – Sometimes you want to cry, sometimes you want to yell, but it is not healthy for your kids to witness these kinds of displays. They may come to associate your work with unpleasantness. Wear a brave face in front of the kids then go off alone where you can express your emotions without restraint.

7. When you work, work. When you play, play. – Don't be answering emails while you are watching a movie with the kids, putting up the Christmas tree, or singing 'Happy Birthday'.

8. Get your family involved with your work – You can put stamps on postcards, preview houses, put in lawn signs, and a host of other things with your spouse and/or kids. Bring them into your business so they feel some ownership.

Key Takeaway

Even if you can do well without the support of your family, why would you want to? What good is it to become a top producer if you alienate the ones you love in the process? Get everyone rowing in the same direction. You will be happier, your family will be happier, and you will sell more houses.

#10

9 Survival Tips For
Real Estate Spouses

It is not easy being married to a real estate agent. It is not a normal life. My wife has walked every step of my career alongside me. She offers some tips that only one who has lived the life could know.

1. Real estate sales is not a job, it is a lifestyle – and not a normal one at that– If you expect regular hours, weekends free, evenings (and vacations) without phone interruptions, and a regular paycheck every week, you are in for a shock.

2. You are going to experience a rollercoaster ride – You can't work in real estate and not experience fear, frustration, exhilaration, desperation, and more. This is what your spouse is experiencing and this is what you will experience. In many cases there will not be a support system at the office so <u>you</u> are the support system.

3. Don't spend all the money you make – You may have a fat commission check now but not see another payday for two months. Budget.

4. Put money aside for taxes – It's easy to forget to do this but the IRS does not forget. Put 20% of every check into an account to pay your taxes. Tap into it if you must pay a bill, but it is easier to be aware of your tax obligation if you 'borrow' from this fund.

5. If your spouse just wants to veg when she gets home, let her – She may not want to talk about her day just yet, especially if she was interacting with others all day.

6. Adopt the attitude, "Easy come, easy go" – Deals will fall apart and you'll think you lost $5,000. Then a deal will come together and you'll think you gained $5,000. Don't assign too much importance to a single deal.

7. Dinner (and other events) may sometimes be delayed – Your spouse is not doing this on purpose. Sometimes a call runs long or someone has to see a house 'right now'. An agent's schedule is very fluid. This can be frustrating but this has an upside as well. You can often attend your kid's daytime events or have an impromptu breakfast or lunch with your spouse during the workweek.

8. Understand that this is a business and business needs investment capital – It may not be a lot but there may be times you need to spend money you have not yet earned to generate leads that will provide future revenues. It's not spending; it is investing.

9. The best thing you can do to help your real estate agent spouse is support them – Help them feel good about themselves. Encourage them. Their success is your success!

11 Reasons A Career In Real Estate Sales Can Be Awesome

The purpose of the next two lists is to illustrate how the very reason one agent loves being a real estate agent is the reason another hates it. The reasons are the same. What's different is how each is interpreted. Here's how agents that love the business see things.

1. Your income is not fixed - Unlike a salaried job where you make the same every year, in real estate there is no limit to how much you can make.

2. You are an independent contractor - You are your own boss and call your own shots with little oversight from a superior.

3. It requires no special education - You have to pass a licensing exam of course, but beyond that you don't need a college or even a high school degree. Practically anyone can become a real estate agent.

4. Your workday schedule is up to you - You alone decide when you will work.

5. You work with people - You often become part of their family and help share with them in one of the great joys of their lives, i.e. helping them establish their home.

6. Every day is different – No two days are alike. When you awake each day you have no idea what opportunities and successes await you.

7. Your success is up to you - Your income is exactly what you deserve.

8. Every day presents new challenges – You're constantly challenged, always looking to find solutions to a never-ending parade of problems. It can be exhilarating.

9. If the pressure gets too great, you can take a day off - It's called a mental health day and you don't have to ask permission to have one.

10. It's an exciting lifestyle, not a job – Real estate becomes part of you. You never shut it off.

11. People depend on you - Oftentimes your client's future depends on you. It is an awesome privilege.

11 Reasons A Career In
Real Estate Sales Can Be Awful

Not everyone is cut out to be a real estate agent. Here's how they view the aspects of the business.

1. Your income is not fixed - Unlike a salaried job where you are assured of making the same every year, it is possible in real estate to make far less, or even nothing at all.

2. You are an independent contractor - You call your own shots with little oversight from a boss. No oversight can leave you clueless as to what to do next.

3. It requires no special education – Practically anyone can be a real estate agent. You don't even need a high school diploma to be a real estate agent. Unfortunately you are often called on to work with colleagues with little or no education or training.

4. Your workday schedule is up to you - You and you alone decide when you will work. Many people, given this freedom, choose not to work at all.

5. You work with people – You get to deal with anxious people who are going through one of the most stressful events in their life and who take their frustrations out on you.

6. Every day is different – Each new day offers the possibility of being worse than the day before.

7. Your success is up to you - Your income is exactly what you deserve. This may not be good.

8. Every day presents new challenges – There is no escape from a never-ending parade of problems. It can be overwhelming.

9. If the pressure gets too great, you can take the day off - It's called a mental health day and you don't have to ask anyone's permission to take one. Without discipline though, 'mental health days' can easily become the norm (see items # 2 and 4 on this list)

10. It's an exciting lifestyle, not a job – Real estate becomes part of you. You can't escape it.

11. People depend on you - In some respects your client's future depends on you. You may not want that responsibility.

Section 2

———◆———

Day-to-Day Operations

Matt Williams

#13

27 Items Every Real Estate Agent Should Have In Her Car

Because real estate is so fast-paced, you need to be ready for any possibility. 'Be Prepared' is the Boy Scout motto. It's a great motto for real estate agents as well. Sometimes your preparation (or lack thereof) may be the difference between making a sale and not making a sale. Here are 27 must-have items in the real estate agent's car.

1. **A supply of purchase offers.**

2. **Half a dozen pens** – All of which write.

3. **A solar-powered calculator** (Yes I know, your cell phone already has a calculator, but what if your cell phone goes dead or you forget or lose it?)

4. **At least 50 business cards** – You never know when you might get invited to a networking meeting.

5. **Your office's listing packet** – Everything you need to list a home.

6. **A pristine copy of your pre-listing package** – You never know when you might be called in for a listing opportunity that comes from out of the blue.

7. **A paper version of your listing presentation** – Maybe you prefer the paper version or maybe it's just a backup in case your tablet or laptop does not work.

8. **Maps** – Yes I know, you have a GPS on your windshield and another app on your smartphone. Nevertheless, have an atlas of the local area.

9. **GPS** – There is no excuse for getting lost on your way to an appointment or for being late because you miscalculated the time it would take to get there.

10. **Toilet paper** – You'll probably never use it but you'll be glad you have it should the need arise.

11. **A bottle of water** – A properly hydrated real estate agent is a clearer thinking agent.

12. **Energy bars** – Clients play off your energy. Be sure yours is high.

13. **A can of WD-40** – Very handy to quiet squeaky doors. It is also useful for sticky locks.

14. **Can of air freshener** – Spend a few bucks more and get a quality product. There's no point in being cheap and replacing one bad odor with another.

15. **Spare lockboxes** – You never know when one of your existing lockboxes will break and you need to replace it.

16. **Phone book** - Yes I know, you have a smart phone… You may never use it but if you ever need it, you'll be glad you have it. It's also useful for finding businesses from the Yellow Pages.

17. **First aid kit** – Be sure it includes bandages, first aid cream, tweezers, aspirin.

18. **Umbrella** – Carry two so you can offer one to your client in the event of an unexpected cloudburst.

19. **A voice recorder** – You're on your way to an appointment and you ride past a FSBO. Making it easy to capture the phone number means you'll never miss it.

20. **A little drawstring bag of quarters** – Do you have a mug or cup you put your pocket change into every day? Take the

quarters and put them in a little bag in your car. You will then have money for vending machines, car washes, or tolls.

21. **For sale by owner marketing piece** – You can leave it at the FSBO's door whenever you come across one.

22. **A good quality flashlight** – You don't have to spend a lot – $15 will buy you all you need.

23. **A book** – For while waiting for your clients to show.

24. **Supply of your personal brochures** – You never know when you may meet a prospect. Be prepared.

25. **A pair of boots or pullover rubbers** – For those muddy construction sites.

26. **A small tool kit** – Screwdriver, adjustable wrench, hammer, and pliers.

27. **Duct tape** – I've used duct tape to keep a cabinet door closed at an open house, secure a broken for sale sign frame, and fix a fallen cuff on my slacks. It's not for permanent solutions but it's great in a fix. (Zip ties are also useful for broken signs)

It may seem like a lot but virtually everything will fit into a 10-gallon tub that you can secure with a lid and stow away in the trunk of your car.

Matt Williams

14

13 Service Providers That Should Be Part of Your Team

No deal has ever taken place that did not involve a team of service professionals. One of the things your clients expect when they hire you is your recommendation for these needed services. You want to have established relationships with honest, capable, and dependable professionals in each of the following service fields so that you can set your clients up with professionals that will provide the services they need.

1. **Mortgage professional** – Look for an attentive, dependable professional with a hunger for getting loans approved.

2. **Attorney** – I prefer someone even-tempered with a good sense of humor. Also, who always takes my calls.

3. **House inspector** – You want someone who is not an alarmist. He/she also needs to be available on short notice.

4. **Radon testing company**

5. **Moving company**

6. **Insurance broker**

7. **Asbestos/mold removal company**

8. **Oil tank removal expert**

9. **Surveyor** – Besides mapping properties, surveyors are also helpful correcting flood plain designation mistakes.

10. **Mobile home finance company**

11. **Title company**

12. **Junk removal company**

13. **General handyman** – Someone who can fix anything and is available on short notice.

Key Takeaway

It's always a good idea to recommend more than one and let your client decide. If you are handing out a list be sure to have these words on the top of the page, **"Below is a list of service provides other clients have used and reported satisfactory results. You are free to use these or any other you like."**

15

9 Apps You Should
Have on Your Smartphone

The smartphone has revolutionized real estate. As long as you're connected to your network, there is virtually nothing you would need to know for a client that you can't find out immediately. Not only that, but there are hundreds of useful apps that can make your job easier and provide your clients with the information they need to make good decisions. Here are 9 that every real estate agent should have on her phone.

1. **Google Maps** – You may prefer a different mapping program. That's fine. Just be sure to have one that is current and operates in real time.

2 **TurboScan** – This is a simple, easy to use scanning app. You will wonder how you ever got along without it.

3. **NOAA Weather** - I hate weather apps that are bogged down with advertising. All I want to know is whether it's going to be raining three hours from now. This app does that well.

4. **Glympse** - This app tracks where you are. You can send a text to a friend and they will see your location in real time.

5. **Compass** – Not just for finding your way, a compass is also useful for determining the orientation of a house.

6. **Kindle/Audible** – Load a few books for when you are waiting for a client to show up for an appointment.

7. **Trulia/Zillow/Realtor.com** – Must haves for any real estate professional.

8. **Google Translate** – If you are not multi-lingual this app may help you communicate with those you encounter for whom English is not their first language.

9. **Mortgage Calculator** – There are many but I like the ease of use of QL Calc, the free mortgage calculator from Quicken Loans.

16

9 Ways to Make a Great First Impression

It is cliché but it is true, you only get one opportunity to make a great first impression. With so much competition for the attention of prospects, the smart real estate agent will do everything in her power to make a great first impression so the prospect doesn't feel they need to look for another agent. Here are 9 things you can do to make a great first impression.

1. **Dress professionally** – Don't worry about intimidating a seller, it is better to dress too professionally than not professionally enough. Pressed slacks, shined shoes, a sport coat and tie for the men – smart professional outfit for the women, will tip the odds in your favor.

2. **Be on time** – There is no excuse, absolutely no excuse, for not being on time for an appointment. Plan to arrive 15 minutes early to account for traffic. If you have to wait, that's fine. Read your email on your smart phone or a book you've downloaded or just mentally prepare yourself for what you are about to do. It is better to be 30 minutes too early than 30 seconds too late.

3. **Be aware of your presence** – Stand tall and erect, smile, offer a professional handshake, look your prospects directly in the eye.

4. **Address your prospects by their name** – You say you're not good with names? Then get good with names. Take a memory course, read a book, it's not hard. You'll be surprised how much more confident you'll be when you can remember someone's name and recall it at will.

5. **Control the situation** – Prospects buy confidence. If you demonstrate confidence (not cockiness) you will begin to earn

trust right away. That trust will translate into loyalty. If you lead the process skillfully, your prospect will follow your direction.

6. **If you don't know something, admit it** - Honesty goes a long way in developing a great first impression. You're better off confessing that you do not know an answer than to try to bluff your way through. You may think you can pull off a good bluff, but clients know when they're being misled. Having said that…

7. **Know your stuff** – It's okay if you don't know the train schedule, but if you're showing the house and someone asks you the age of the roof, you'd better know it if it is your listing. Nothing says incompetence like an agent who can't answer simple questions about her listing.

8. **Do what you say you are going to do** – The first impression extends beyond your first meeting if you said you were going to do something (email another listing, find out information, etc.). Be certain to follow up promptly. Clients will appreciate that.

9. **Follow-up, follow-up, follow-up** – You may not think so, but most customers respect a professional. By following up, even if the prospect didn't ask for anything, you are establishing yourself as a real estate professional worthy of respect. More often than not this creates a positive impression in the prospect's mind.

17

10 Steps To Making Great Decisions

Perhaps the single greatest factor in determining success or failure in a person's life is their ability to make good decisions. One of the primary responsibilities of the real estate agent is to help her client make good decisions. Here are 10 things you can do to make better decisions for yourself and for your client.

1. **Understand first what the end goal is** - What are you trying to accomplish? What does success look like? The more clearly you can envision what a successful outcome looks like, the better able you will be to make decisions that will achieve it.

2. **Write down every possible choice you have that may result in the desired outcome** - No possibility, no idea is too foolish or too impractical at this point. What you're looking for is to have all your options before you.

3. **Thoroughly evaluate each option** - For each option you have written in Step #2, write down the positives and negatives as well as your best estimate of the likelihood of each happening.

4. **Eliminate those that are clearly inferior to the others** - If there are options on your list where the negatives are far greater than other options on your list, cross them out.

6. **Seek the opinion of someone you trust** - At this time it is wise to bring in a trusted friend or colleague to discuss the options. Take the time to present each option on your narrowed list to someone you trust and ask for their input.

7. **Look inside yourself** - Take some time alone and see if your conscience is nudging you in any particular direction. Listen to your conscience.

8. **Make your decision** - If there is a second option that you decided was good but not as good as your first choice, keep it in mind; you might need a Plan B.

9. **Implement your decision and monitor its consequences closely** - If this choice does not turn out like you thought it would, it is better to understand that early when the consequences may be minor than later when the consequences may be more severe.

10. **Keep a journal of the decisions you make** – In doing so you can maintain a record of which processes worked and which ones could have been done better. This will make you a better decision-maker.

18

7 Situations Where Emailing May Be Better Than Calling

Nothing beats a face-to-face meeting but sometimes that's not possible. So we rely on the telephone, text, and email. In most cases talking to a person is the best form of communication, but sometimes email is better. Here are some of those times.

1. **When you have news that may not be pleasing to your client and you know them to have a hot temper** - If you call them, their emotions may take over and they may not hear another word you say. But if you send a message, even though they may get just as angry, once they've cooled down, they can go back and review what you have written.

2. **When you are making a persuasive argument** – One of the great things about cell phones is you can take calls anywhere. One of the worst things about cellphones is that user can take calls anywhere. You may have an offer that requires some sales skills and if your client is standing in line at the grocery store, they may not hear all you have to say. If you are trying to persuade and/or need the recipient's full attention, email it.

3. **If your client may be "distracted"** – If your client is overwhelmed by work, going through a personal crisis, drinks excessively or for some other reason may not able to give you his complete attention, you might do better to email.

4. **If the message is complex** – If you're communicating the details of an offer, or the items the buyer wants fixed from the engineer's inspection, you do both yourself and your client the greatest service by putting it in email. This way there is no miscommunication.

5. When you are in a significantly different time zone than your message recipient – You could set your alarm for 3 AM but you're probably not going to be at your best, so it's better to use email.

6. If you are accountable to more than one party – Many times we sell homes for estates where there is more than one person involved in the decision. By communicating in email you ensure everyone is getting the same message.

7. When you think there may be trouble later – Nothing puts out the fire of a threatened lawsuit than a paper trail. If you get the sense that your client is someone who has his attorney on speed dial, it may be best to use email for all your material communications.

19

6 Market Statistics You Should Always Have At Your Fingertips

You want to be able to provide your clients with good information so they can make good decisions. You also want to portray yourself as a competent professional – one who knows what's going on. Every month you should make a point to study and know the most recent market statistics in the following categories.

1. **The percentage increase/decrease of closed sales year to date.** - Month by month offers the opportunity for anomalies. Look at the year-over-year comparison of closed sales.

2. **The year to date average sale price** - Average sale prices can be skewed in smaller markets by an unusually high sale, but if you're comparing year over year you can identify trends by knowing the average sale price.

3. **The year-to-date median sale price** - This number shows the general direction the market is moving.

4. **The average days on market** – 'Days on market' is one of the most inaccurate statistics put out by the board of realtors. A house that's been on the market for a year, expires, then comes on with the new agent and sells in one day, shows a 'days on market' of one. In truth it was 366. The number itself is largely useless but inasmuch as it has been measured the same way for years (which means the same inefficiencies have existed for years) you can use the number to measure the trend.

5. **Existing unsold inventory** - Rising inventories means lower prices while declining inventory means rising prices. In order for buyers and sellers to make informed decisions, they need to know which direction the inventory is moving.

6. **Months supply of homes** - Simply take the existing inventory and divided by the most recent month's sales. This number will tell you how long it would take to sell the entire inventory if no other houses came on the market. By itself this stat has little value but over time it offers a useful indication of where the market is heading.

Although not a market statistic, you also want to know the current interest rates as well as the trend.

Key Takeaway

You want to help your clients be successful. Success comes, in part, from making good decisions. Good decisions come from good information. Be sure you know the information your clients need to make good decisions.

20

7 Reasons You Should Not Negotiate Your Fee

It is inevitable that some day a seller is going to ask you to reduce your fee in order to get the listing or make the deal. The temptation may be to give in. Sometimes reducing your fee is the wisest course of action. Most times it is not. Here are 7 reasons you should not reduce your fee.

1. **It may be a test** - The seller may be testing you see what kind of sales person you are. If you cave on your fee the seller may conclude that you will also cave when negotiating on his behalf.

2. **It's not fair to your other clients who pay your full fee** - What does it say about the integrity of your business when you do something for one client that you won't do for another?

3. **It creates a slippery slope** - The first time you're asked to discount your fee ½%. You agree to the reduction. The next time it's ¾%. The time after that 1%. Where does it stop?

4. **Your revenues are decreased** - Your fee is your source of revenues, the lifeblood of your business. Revenues should be respected and protected.

5. **Agents talk and they talk to sellers** - If you develop a reputation as one who will cut his fee, you may find it costing you in a competitive listing situation. You may get the listing but if the losing agent knows that you discount, she may say to the seller "Be sure to get that discounted fee".

6. **Giving in is a habit** - As with any habit it becomes the norm over time. Make your norm that you are paid your full fee – whatever it is.

7. **Think about what it is you are really doing** – If, instead of simply agreeing to a 1% reduction in your fee for that $300,000 sale, you thought of it as going to the bank, withdrawing $3,000, and giving it to the seller, you might think differently of what you have been asked to do.

21

6 Situations Where (Maybe) You Should Discount Your Fee

For most agents, the commission they receive on sales is their only source of revenue. For that reason they must respect the need to protect their fee. In most cases discounting your fee is not wise but there are occasions when it may be appropriate. Here are some of those occasions:

1. **When reducing the fee makes possible a transaction that triggers another transaction** – You have a listing and your seller is buying another house with you once their house sells. By making the first sale possible, you get the second.

2. **When there is a true hardship for the seller** – A serious illness, death, or overseas deployment may leave a seller hurting. You may be able to lessen their pain by working for a little less.

3. **When your fee is the difference between making the deal and not making a deal <u>and</u> the request is reasonable** – The buyer and seller are at an impasse over $1,000. You and the other agent kicking in can make the deal happen. You may not feel good about it but it may be the smart thing to do.

4. **When you are doing multiple transactions for the same client** – Some examples are a builder with a new subdivision, an investor liquidating his portfolio, or a lender giving you their foreclosed properties.

5. **As a professional courtesy to a dedicated service provider** – For example, an attorney refers you a lot of clients. It is not inappropriate to offer a discounted fee for the attorney when she sells her house with you.

6. **For a loyal repeat customer** – When someone has been loyal to you and referred you to many of their friends, you can show your gratitude by offering a discount on your next deal with them.

22

6 Dialogues When You Have To Deliver Bad News

There are times real estate agents need to have tough conversations with their clients. It may be to lower the price, contradict them or simply tell them something they don't want to hear. It's difficult for the agent because what we may have to say could be interpreted by our client the wrong way. They may think we are not working for them or in their best interests. A good way to deliver bad news is to have a practiced sentence or two to create a climate that allows you to speak honestly and frankly. Here are six dialogues that will help you deliver bad news:

1. **"Well this is a conversation I wish we didn't have to have, (pause) but we need to talk about . . ."**

2. **"I don't want you to get mad at me, but I also don't want you to come back to me later saying 'You knew what I was doing was wrong – why didn't you try to stop me'?**

3. **"I'm kind of in a tough position here. I have a dilemma – do I tell you the truth and risk having you get mad at me or do I mislead you and keep you happy with me?"**

4. **"Let me ask you a question – if I thought you were about to do something wrong, something that would be detrimental to you, would you want me to tell you?"**

5. **"I don't want you to do anything you don't want to do, but as your agent I have a responsibility to protect you if I think you are about to do something that is not in your best interest. I think you are about to do something not in your best interest. May I tell you what it is?"**

6. "Sometimes my job is very difficult because of conversations like I am about to have with you. Can I tell you what I mean?"

Key Takeaway

Taking the edge off your difficult conversation by beginning with a degree of humility and vulnerability will often be the difference between your client hearing what you have to say and them being so upset they hear nothing. Choose your words carefully.

23

12 Steps For Dealing With An Angry Client

It will happen. Someday you are going to be confronted by an angry client. Their anger may be justified or not, but these situations not only are trying, they must be handled deftly in order to preserve the relationship. When you have an angry client lashing out at you, remember these 12 steps.

1. Understand that they are upset – You may not think the issue rises to the level that they do. You may not understand why they are so upset. But if you dismiss their concerns as trivial, you are off to a bad start. Be sensitive to the fact they are upset.

2. Commit to not making a bad situation worse – Take a deep breath, dial back your own emotions, and decide right then and there that you are not going to pour gasoline on a fire. That never helps.

3. Empathize with them – "I understand that you are upset. I don't blame you."

4. Let them talk – They need to talk. Talking allows them to be heard, which is mostly what they want.

5. Don't interrupt – Talking is also going to help calm them down (eventually). Don't do anything to interfere with that.

6. Don't contradict – at least not yet – Listen until they are done.

7. Take notes – As they rant, jot down the issues that you want to address.

8. When it seems they are done ask if you can talk – "Is there anything else you want to add before I address your issue?"

9. Verify that you understand what is upsetting them – Most angry people want to be heard and understood. Tell them you think you understand what the issue is (if you do) but you would like to make sure. Then, repeat what you believe are the issues that need attention.

10. Explain your position – If you need to explain or shed additional light on the subject, now is the time to do it

11. Ask what you can do to help – Make certain they know you care about resolving the issue.

12. Empathize with them – Again, let them know you understand that they are upset, you understand why, and you are committed to making things right.

24

7 Things You Can Do To Avoid Being Sued

Whether you win in court or not is not the issue – if you are sued, you lose. The time spent preparing your defense and giving depositions, the money paid to attorneys, and the stress all make you a loser even if you don't lose in court. While you can't guarantee never being sued, there are steps you can take that will minimize the likelihood. Here are 7.

1. **Don't practice law** – Unless you are an attorney, do not give legal advice. Direct those questions to those who are trained in the law.

2. **Don't make decisions for your clients** – You can give them options (and you should) but have them make the decision. The minute you make up their mind for them, you own the outcome . . . and its consequences.

3. **Be the resource, not the source** – Tell, show, or direct your clients to where they can get the information they need, don't provide it yourself. If you make a mistake in relaying the information or if you pass along incorrect information someone gave you, you may be the one responsible for the consequences.

4. **Memorize this dialogue, "That's a good question for your attorney"** – It bears repeating, don't practice law unless you are an attorney.

5. **Keep good notes as well as copies of all emails, text messages, and correspondence** – You may be sued but if you can share evidence that clearly exonerates you, it is likely that will be the end of it.

6. **Never start a sentence that begins, "Now, I'm not an attorney, but . . . "** - The person you are talking to will claim to have never heard the first six words but will remember exactly everything else you said . . . and they will take it as legal advice. If you don't walk anywhere near the edge of the cliff, you don't have to fear falling off the cliff. Don't offer anything that looks or sounds like advice that should come from their attorney.

7. **Don't act outside your authority** – The buyer wants to move a few things into the vacant house two days before closing and they ask you if it's okay. That's not within your authority. If you don't know how far your authority extends, err on the side of caution.

25

7 Reasons To Fire A Client

It does not happen often but there are occasions when firing a client may be appropriate. You don't want to have a hair trigger, firing every client that rubs you the wrong way (after all, real estate is a contact sport), but there are certain actions and behaviors that warrant sending a client on his way. Here are 7.

1. **They ask you to do something illegal** – No client, no matter how large the potential fee, is worth losing your license for.

2. **They treat you disrespectfully** – They habitually show up late or cancel at the last minute, use vulgar language in your presence, talk down to you, yell at you, or generally treat you in a disrespectful manner.

3. **They treat others disrespectfully** – I recall a husband and wife I was showing houses to and the husband called his wife 'stupid'. That was enough for me. I felt bad for the wife but it's my choice to allow that man into my life. I chose not to.

4. **They consistently reject your counsel** – If your counsel is sound and they refuse to follow it, this venture is probably not going to end well. You might do well to move on with your life without them in it.

5. **They insist on unreasonable demands** – You took the listing at a price you thought too high, no buyer or agent has shown the slightest interest in it, and now the seller wants to raise the price $100,000. It might be best to let them go.

6. **They won't work to your standards** – The buyer refuses to provide evidence of a pre-approval. The seller refuses a 'for sale' sign, open house, or some other action you need from them to sell the house. Compromising your standards compromises your business.

7. **They don't do what they say they will do** – The relationship between a real estate agent and the client is essentially a partnership. To some degree, each depends on the other. When one partner consistently proves himself or herself to be undependable, it's time to end the partnership.

26

8 Ways To Deal With
Rejection And Disappointment

There is no getting around the fact that rejection and disappointment are part of the real estate sales business. Being able to deal with disappointment is critical to success as a real estate agent. Here are 8 ways to keep disappointment and rejection from holding you back.

1. **Remember you are not alone** – You are part of a brother/sister hood that experiences disappointment all the time. It is simply a part of what we do. In fact as you read this, somewhere a real estate agent is being rejected.

2. **Each rejection makes you stronger** - In time, disappointments will roll off your back, but only as a result of having endured previous disappointments.

3. **Don't take it personally** – If you've done your best yet still lost, remember that no one wins them all. Heck, in baseball if you fail to get a hit 7 times out of 10 you probably end up in the Hall of Fame.

4. **Learn from the experience** – Use the occasion to ensure you did all you could. And if you didn't do all you could, resolve right there and then to never let that happen again. One of the best listings in my career is one I didn't get. But I realized what I had done wrong and never made that mistake again ensuring I would get more listings in the future.

5. **Review your business plan goals** – Losing one opportunity does not ruin an entire year. Take a look at your goals, realize that you are still on track, take a deep breath, and focus on the future.

6. **Call a favorite past customer** – Just call to say 'Hi'. Five minutes on the phone with one of your satisfied clients may be just what you need to put that disappointment in its proper perspective.

7. **Go to the gym, go for a walk, ride your bike, punch a heavy bag** – A little physical exertion will feel good and allow you to work off some of that negative energy.

8. **Get back to work** – Don't let one disappointment hold you back from future successes. You'll recover quicker if you dive right back into work.

27

36 Books From My
Bookshelf You Might Find Helpful

It has been said that a year from now you will be the same person you are today except the books you read and the people you meet. Reading is a great way to expand your knowledge. If you don't enjoy reading, many of these books are available in audiobook form. You can find each one of these on Amazon.com. Many can be purchased used for a few dollars.

1. *The Memory Book* by Harry Lorayne and Jerry Lucas – Who couldn't use some help with their memory? This book will help.

2. *How I Raised Myself From Failure to Success In Selling* by Frank Bettger – An inspirational story of overcoming failure.

3. *Life is Tremendous* by Charlie 'Tremendous' Jones – Read anything by Charlie Jones and you will feel better.

4. *A Nation of Realtors* by Jeffrey M. Hornstein – If you are into the history of our profession you will enjoy Hornstein's book.

5. *The Magic of Thinking Big* by David J. Schwartz – A classic.

6. *The Art of the Deal* by Donald J. Trump – Love him or hate him, it doesn't change the fact he is a dealmaker. You can learn from his experiences.

7. *Lessons From My Brother Zig* by Floyd Wickman and Mary H. Johnson – Floyd Wickman writing about Zig Ziglar. It doesn't get much better than that.

8. *In His Steps* by Charles M Sheldon – A century old classic that shows what happens when you dedicate yourself to a life of service.

9. *The Houses That Sears Built* by Rosemary Thornton – A fascinating look at how houses were sold in the early part of the 20th Century.

10. *Houses By Mail* by Catherine Cole Stephenson and H. Ward Jandl – Another interesting look at 'mail order houses'.

11. *50 Years With the Golden Rule* by J.C. Penney – He built an empire from a single small store. Inspirational.

12. *It's Easier to Succeed Than To Fail* by S. Truett Cathy – The founder of Chik-fil-A shares his story and his system for success.

13. *10 Greatest Salespersons – What They Say About Selling* by Robert L. Shook – Learning about the lives of successful people is always good. Here are the stories of 10 successful salespeople.

14. *The Time Trap* by Alec McKenzie – We all have the same amount of time. Those who use it wisely accomplish more. This book shows you how.

15. *See You at the Top* by Zig Ziglar – Ziglar's first and, I think, his best. A classic.

16. *Man's Search For Meaning* by Viktor Frankel – Concentration camp survivor offers powerful insight into what is important in life.

17. *Salesman of the Century* by Ron Popeil – You know him as the infomercial guy ("Set it and forget it") but his story is inspiring and informative.

18. ***Think and Grow Rich*** by Napoleon Hill – What are the habits of the world's most successful business people? Hill tells you in this classic.

19. ***The Power of Positive Thinking*** by Norman Vincent Peale – As relevant today as it was 60 years ago.

20. ***How to Win Friends and Influence People*** by Dale Carnegie – Millions have been influenced by Carnegie. This is his all-time classic.

21. ***Tough Times Never Last But Tough People Do*** by Robert H Schuller – Practical advice for dealing with life.

22. ***The Greatest Salesman in the World*** by Og Mandino – Floyd Wickman once told me that if an agent is in a slump the first thing he should do is read this book. Enough said.

23. ***How to Sell Anything to Anybody*** by Joe Girard – Girard sold more than 1,400 cars in a single year. You can learn from him.

24. ***The 7 Habits of Highly Effective People*** – Stephen Covey – One of the all-time classics.

25. ***Dress For Success*** – John T. Molloy – The way you look has meaning. This book shows you how to have your clothes work for, and not against, you.

26. ***Who Moved My Cheese*** – by Spencer Johnson – Nothing stays the same is the lesson of this best-selling book.

27. ***The Big Book of Real Estate Ads*** – by William Pivar and Bradley Pivar – I've worn out my copy. Great for writing vivid descriptions.

28. ***Get Motivated*** by Tamara Lowe – A fascinating motivational book that focuses on your individual personality traits.

29. *Walk Like a Giant, Sell Like a Madman* by Ralph R. Roberts – Practical sales advice from one of real estate's most successful salespeople.

30. *The Challenge* by Robert Allen – If you have the desire you can do anything, as Allen demonstrates with this true story.

31. *As A Man Thinketh* by James Allen – Change your thoughts and you change your life. An all-time classic.

32. *The Go-Getter* by Peter B. Kyne – Written nearly 100 years ago, this is the story that demonstrates what it takes to succeed.

33. *Planning For Success in Real Estate Sales* by Matt Williams – You'll sell more houses if you work from an effective plan. This book shows you how to create and implement that plan.

34. *How To Talk to Anyone, Anytime, Anywhere* by Larry King – King is the best at getting people to talk – a key skill for salespeople. Here he teaches his methods for getting people to relax and reveal.

35. *Good To Great* by Jim Collins – How do you go from successful to super-successful? Collins shares the stories and methods of some who have done it.

36. *Holy Bible* – The best-selling book of all time is a great sales training book as well.

Section 3

—•—

Your Office

Matt Williams

28

12 Things Great Brokers Do

There's no question the agent is the one who is responsible for his own success, but his path can be made straighter and smoother if he works with a great broker. Here are 12 things a broker should be doing to help make his agents more successful.

1. Care about the agent's success – A broker that cares if his agent is successful – by whatever way the agent defines success – is a broker who will go the extra mile to teach, encourage, and challenge the agent.

2. Create a healthy work environment – A toxic environment of backstabbing, infighting, and chaos isn't good for anyone. A good broker works to create a cooperative environment and does not tolerate toxic agents.

3. Attract quality agents – When great agents join a company they bring their energy, enthusiasm, ideas, and experience to the company. It's all good.

4. Set a good example – Whether it means being on time, dressing well, treating others with respect, or not tolerating nonsense, what the broker <u>does</u> means far more than what the broker <u>says</u>.

5. Hold to strict standards – A broker that tolerates dysfunction, dishonesty, or unethical behavior is, in effect, saying that type of behavior is acceptable. It should come as no surprise then when that behavior runs rampant through the office.

6. Stand up for their agents - The customer is NOT always right. A good broker will always investigate complaints made against his agents, but when the facts show the agent was acting properly, he will stand up to the accuser and explain where they are wrong.

7. Keep the agents informed – One of the agent's responsibilities is to help their client make good decisions. One way we help with that is by providing good data. The broker should be providing market stats, local news and the trends that affect the real estate market.

8. Treat agents equally – There's nothing wrong with a broker having different feelings for different agents, but all agents should be afforded respect, protection, and the help they need to succeed.

9. Stand up to their agents – The agent is NOT always right. The broker needs to stand up to the agent when that agent needs correction, even if that agent is your top producer and even if the correction upsets the agent.

10. Lead the office – The strongest personality in the office is the leader of that office. It should be the broker. Sometimes it is not. Sometimes it is an agent or staff employee.

11. Celebrate successes – Good brokers do this publically. Reaching a sales milestone like $100,000 in commissions, reading aloud letters of praise, or sharing a story of exemplary work all serve to make the agent feel respected while at the same time showing the other agents what they should be striving for.

12. Always look for new ways to help his agents – The broker's job is to help the agents. A good broker is always searching for ways to do this.

4 Misguided Reasons For Joining a Particular Real Estate Company

Joining the wrong company is one of the major reasons agents fail. All companies are not the same. Agents must do a thorough job of research before committing to a particular real estate company. Here are four bad reasons for joining a particular real estate company.

1. **It is the office closest to your home** – Once upon a time when agents went to the office every day this might have had some influence on what company you should join. But now, with agents rarely coming to the office, the proximity to your home has little importance.

2. **You just bought a house using that agency and they said you would be a good real estate agent** – They may be a great company and the right place for you, but base that on what they offer in terms of training and support, not the fact that they sold you a house.

3. **They offer you the highest split** – 80% may sound like a great split but 80% of zero dollars is zero. Companies that offer commission splits well outside the norm often do so because they have little else to offer – no training and no support. Beware of companies that make you an offer that seems too good to be true.

4. **They are the biggest name company in the area** – A well-known strategy employed by many companies is to have "the largest army", i.e. the most agents. Quality takes a back seat to quantity and the company's focus is on recruiting and not agent development. Bigger does not always mean better.

Matt Williams

30 Things You Can Do To Make Your Office A Better Place

Nobody wants to work in a dysfunctional office. Here are 30 things you can do to make your office a better place for everyone.

1. **If you see trash on the floor, pick it up and throw it away.**

2. **Don't hog the computers** – I knew a broker who had his shared computers placed on platforms that required the agent to stand in order to use it. This made it uncomfortable for the agent and made sure no one hogged the computer.

3. **Don't download software on the office computers without the permission of the office manager** – A virus that incapacitates the computer will not make you a popular agent with your colleagues.

4. **Don't come to the office dressed unprofessionally** – You may not be meeting with anyone that day but your colleagues may. Show them courtesy and respect by not coming in shabby, dirty, unprofessional attire.

5. **When you're done using the conference room clean up after yourself** - Leave it better than you got it for the next agent.

6. **Don't eat or drink someone else's food in the refrigerator.**

7. **Don't leave food in the refrigerator beyond its freshness date.**

8. **If you see some supply item getting low, let the office manager know.**

9. **Don't engage in gossip** – It is unproductive, unprofessional, and the source of many problems in offices.

10. **Don't take the parking spot closest to the front door -** Leave it for customers.

11. **Never use foul language in the office.**

12. **If you refer a client to an agent in your office, make sure the referral is in writing** – You show great respect to your colleague when you insist on eliminating any possibility of any misunderstanding by having your agreement in writing.

13. **If you smoke outside the office don't leave your butts piled up on the ground.**

14. **Don't waste other agent's time.**

15. **Treat every person who walks through your door as if they were your own customer.**

16. **Never criticize a colleague in public** – If you have something critical to say about someone in your office, find a private place, close the door, and do it respectfully.

17. **Support your colleagues by taking part in the tour of new listings** - Don't attend only when you have a house on the tour.

18. **Attend (and be on time for) your office meeting.**

19. **If you come across an inspiring message or useful article, share it with your office mates** – But don't overdo it.

20. **Never promote yourself at the expense of your fellow associates** – If you can't characterize your successes without putting down – implied or real – the other agents in your office, don't do it at all.

21. **When you see a new agent in your office, give them a word of encouragement** – Remember how you felt when you were new.

22. **Congratulate success. Console disappointment.**

23. **Don't complain about things** – If you see a problem, work on coming up with a solution.

24. **Never fan the flames or pour gasoline on the fire of a bad situation.**

25. **Treat your colleagues the same way you would treat a client.**

26. **Knock before entering a closed door.**

27. **Every so often make a point to thank the office manager** – Perhaps the toughest job in real estate is being responsible for the operation of the office. Let your administrator know you appreciate the work she does for you.

28. **If someone is eating lunch or dinner at their desk, let them eat in peace.**

29. **Demonstrate a good attitude always** – If you're having a bad attitude day, either take it home, hide it behind a closed door, or change.

30. **Work together as a team** – Remember T-E-A-M means Together Each Achieves More.

Matt Williams

Section 4

———◆———

Getting Listings

Matt Williams

12 Sources of Names For Your Sphere of Influence (or Book of Business) List

According to the National Association of Realtors, the overwhelming majority of Americans do not know a real estate agent. A primary focus for you then should be to make certain that the people in your life know you are a real estate agent. A system for working your sphere of influence should be part of every agent's business. Ideally this list should consist of approximately 200 names. Here's where you can find those names.

1. **Your neighborhood** – Make sure those you live near know you as more than 'the guy with the pickup truck' or the 'woman who walks the labradoodle'.

2. **Past clients** - It's not just their business you want but the business of those in their sphere of influence as well.

3. **Buyers of homes that you had listed** – You had the listing and another agent sold it. That buyer should be on your list. They may have been unhappy with their agent or their agent may be gone from the business when the time comes to sell.

4. **Membership lists of organizations you belong to** – A no-brainer. Being part of the same organization fosters trust.

5. **Your address book** – There may be a friend you haven't talked with (or even thought of) in a while but who needs a trusted real estate agent.

6. **Your Christmas card list** – Even people who already moved far away. They may still have friends and family in your market.

7. **The parents of your children's friends.**

8. **Friends from your church, synagogue, or other house of worship.**

9. **Former work colleagues** – Including those who were in the real estate business but are no longer.

10. **Past clients and customers who did not do business with you** – Maybe they didn't buy because their credit needed fixing. Maybe they didn't sell because of a temporary problem. That's no reason to forget them. Stay in touch.

11. **People for whom you are the customer** – Your mechanic, lawn guy, accountant, butcher, etc. You do business with them; they should do business with you . . . or at the very least know what business you are in.

12. **Your children's teachers, coaches, music instructors** – Anyone who is a part of your life and knows you more than in just passing is a candidate for your list.

Key Takeaway

Most people do not know a real estate agent. Make sure the people in your life know that you are one.

31 Ways to Initiate Relationships With People Who Might Have a House To Sell

The essence of any sales business is developing new relationships with people who may need your service. This truth is lost on many agents who believe real estate is about showing houses, negotiating deals, and attending closings. But how do you do any of that if you don't have someone to do it for? Job #1 of the real estate professional is initiating new relationships. It should be at the top of your 'to do' list every day. Here are 31 ways you can initiate new relationships.

1. **Wear your name badge everywhere you go while you are working** – Don't be surprised when a stranger asks 'How's the real estate market?' Your name badge does more than tell your name – it says you are a real estate expert.

2. **Host open houses** – Visitors may have a house to sell. Neighbors who are thinking of selling may drop in too . . . especially if you invite them.

3. **Contact FSBOs** – You already know they want to sell. Most will eventually list with an agent. It won't be you if you don't reach out to them.

4. **Contact expired listings** – They key here is a compelling message coupled with consistency and persistence.

5. **Host informational seminars** – Topics such as 'How to raise the value of your home' or 'How to relocate to a different part of the country' will attract homeowners looking to sell.

6. **Offer a fair trade via direct mail** – "I'll tell you the value of your home or what things you can do to boost its value if you agree to meet with me".

7. **Publish a real estate column in the local weekly newspaper** – Brand yourself as the local real estate expert. There are even companies who will ghost write the columns for you.

8. **Sponsor a writing contest in a local school** – Offer a U.S. Savings Bond to the winner.

9. **Take out business card size ads in club newsletters** – These inexpensive ads are great for reaching sellers who share your interests (if you belong to the club).

10. **Announce every new listing with the 'Just Listed' card** – A great way to get buyer leads too.

11. **Announce every new sale with a 'Just Sold' card** – Still one of the best advertisements for a real estate agent.

12. **Sponsor a local youth team** – Little league, marching band, basketball or any group that needs a financial backer.

13. **Seasonal giveaways** – Balloons at parades, pumpkins at Halloween, etc.

14. **Develop a network of agents in places where people from your area are moving to** – Establish relationships with agents in popular destination markets. Agents there might know early in the relocation process that there will soon be a new listing in your marketplace. Referrals can work both ways.

15. **Rent a booth at tradeshows** – Home shows and kid's expos are both great ways to get face to face with potential home sellers.

16. **Buy or lease a moving van with an advertisement and offer it for free to customers and local community groups** – These are not cheap but parked in front of your office they are like a billboard.

17. **Develop a network of 'bird dogs'** – Encourage your friends and family to actively talk you up to people they know who need to sell.

18. **Make a point to call two people on your sphere of influence list every day** – Call to tell them you were thinking of them. Don't push. Be genuinely interested in them. Ask them if they might know a buyer for your newest listing.

19. **Host a community event** – For example, a blood drive, coat drive, etc. You could offer your office as a drop off spot for a food pantry.

20. **Invest in an Internet ad program.** Many soon-to-be sellers start the process by researching online. Your ad may be just the thing that results in you getting a listing.

21. **Host dinner parties for clients** - If you are fond of entertaining, dinner parties can be a big success. All your guests will have one thing in common, i.e. you are their real estate agent.

22. **Volunteer** – Besides being a good thing to do, delivering meals, coaching a little league team, or organizing a trash pickup day expands your sphere of influence.

23. **Send letters to out of area owners** - A well-timed letter from you inquiring as to whether the absentee owner might consider selling may earn you a listing opportunity.

24. **Visit garage sales** - Oftentimes sellers look to de-clutter before putting their home on the market by hosting a garage sale. Dropping by at the end of the sale (not when they're busy) may afford you the opportunity to discuss the market and what you can do for them.

25. **Wedding announcements/new baby announcements** - Changes in family often precede changes in living arrangements.

26. **Develop a networking group for insurance and legal professionals** - Attorneys often select the agent for their out-of-town clients or estate sellers. Good insurance people are aware of what's going on in their client's lives, including whether there may be a move coming up.

27. **Go door to door** – While knocking on doors may not yield good results (most homeowners are suspicious of strangers who come to their front door), strolling through a neighborhood on a sunny spring Saturday morning when people are out working in their yards may be the spark that turns into a listing opportunity.

28. **Cold call local businesses** - Walk into a local business and ask how you can help them get more customers. Then tell them your business and how they can help you.

29. **Hire a pilot and take aerial photos of attractive houses** - This isn't for every house, and it will involve a bit of an investment but what a door opener for a farm or estate that photographs well from above. Frame them and then mail them to the owner as a special gift from you. Even if they have no interest in selling now you will have made a powerful impression.

30. **Rent billboard** – Billboards aren't cheap but if you have a good location and a brief compelling message i.e. "If I Don't Sell Your House I'll Buy Your House" it can be worth every penny.

31. **Host a local radio program** – Brand yourself as the local expert.

Key Takeaway

There are no bad ways to meet potential clients. Some are better than others but any effort invested in creating new relationships is good. Choose methods that agree with your personality and then be deliberate and consistent in implementing those methods.

33

13 Clues That a Homeowner May Soon Be Putting Their Home on the Market

There are clues sellers leave behind before they put their house on the market. If you are alert to these clues you may be able to identify a prospective listing far in advance of the seller reaching out to an agent. All sellers do not do all these things, but virtually every seller does at least one. Keep your eyes open and you will have more listing opportunities.

1. They have a change in employment – Develop good relationships with professional job recruiters and employment agencies. They often know someone is moving early in the process.

2. A change in family – It could be a new baby, merging of families, or divorce but when family changes there is sometimes a move not far behind.

3. Fix up the house – Keep your eyes open to homeowners making improvements to their home. They may be getting it ready to sell.

4. Attend local open houses – They may be looking for their next home or they may be scouting out the market. Either way you have the chance to develop a relationship with them first if you are hosting an open house they attend.

5. Sell things – De-cluttering is big and many sellers hold garage sales or sell stuff on Craigslist prior to calling in an agent.

6. Call movers – Stay close to the moving companies in your area. They often can alert you to one of those sellers that want everything in place before they list.

7. Contact their attorney – Attorneys are trusted advisors. They often are informed of an impending loss (and the need to sell the parent's home), divorce, foreclosure and more before anyone else.

8. Tell a friend – That friend they tell may be your former client. Stay in touch with your sphere of influence so you are at the top of their mind when the topic of real estate comes up.

9. Fall behind in their mortgage payment – They may not want to admit they are delinquent but you don't have to share that you know. A simple letter to someone in the early stages of foreclosure, asking if they would consider selling, may give you the chance to help someone out of a bad situation.

10. Buy books on selling – Why not offer a free book on selling as part of a direct mail campaign? Someone asking for the book is likely a listing possibility.

11. See their neighbor's house go up for sale – It happens all the time. A house goes on the market and that gets the neighbors thinking of selling too. Just listed cards are a great way to capture these opportunities.

12. Search online – Online ads are expensive but the Internet is often the first place sellers go. You want to be where the sellers are early in the process. That's online.

13. Contact an auction company – Many estates look to auctions as a way to turn unwanted clutter into cash. Staying close to the people involved in the area's local auction houses may give you the inside track on an upcoming listing.

34

10 Steps to Direct Mail Success

It may seem old-fashioned but direct mail still is one of the most effective ways to initiate relationships, especially with sellers. Every real estate agent should have a direct mail system as part of her business plan. Whether you are sending prospecting letters or postcards, here are 10 tips to make your direct mail program most effective.

1. Begin knowing that most of your mail will be thrown away – 1%-2% return on direct mail is considered good. Don't be discouraged when you get few or even no replies to a mailing.

2. Quantify what your investment is likely to return – It is difficult to calculate this amount when you are just starting your program but it will be easier and more accurate after you have done this for some time. The point is you want to know that there is a reason for the investment of time and money.

3. Have a clear, compelling, message - This is not the time to be subtle. You have literally three seconds to grab the reader's attention. Experiment with different messages and stick with the one that gives you the best results.

4. Don't just announce your success – include a call to action - It's good to announce you sold the house down the street but it's even better to offer a free market report too. Make the message relevant to the recipient.

5. Be sure your face, logo, and contact information are obvious – Again, this is not the time to be subtle. Make sure anyone seeing this mailing piece knows it is about real estate.

6. Use Every Door Direct Mail (EDDM) - This outstanding program from the Postal Service allows you to send oversized cards to specific neighborhoods for less than half the cost of first-class postage. It's a no-brainer.

7. If you are working on a tight budget, opt for 'Just Sold' cards rather than 'Just Listed' cards – 'Just Sold 'means you got the job done – a powerful message to potential sellers. Better to send 400 'Just Sold' cards than 200 'Just Listed' and 200 'Just Sold'.

8. Be consistent - As with any other prospecting system the more consistent you are the more successful you will be.

9. Be persistent - Even if you get no response with your first several mailings, don't give up. Direct mail works.

10. Plan your mailings a year in advance - Give careful thought to when the best time to mail is. For example, December is undesirable, as your mailing may get lost in a sea of Christmas cards. January is far better.

35

11 Items That Should Be In Your Pre-Listing Package

The pre-listing package is a marketing piece delivered to your listing prospect in advance of your listing presentation appointment. Its purpose is to predispose sellers to want to use you. This is your opportunity to brag on yourself without appearing boastful. Properly used, a pre-listing package often will win you the listing even before you get to the house. Here's what should be in your pre-listing package.

1. A letter from your broker thanking the seller for considering you – Show the homeowner that you are part of a larger organization and that there is more to you than just you.

2. Your personal one-page brochure – List your credentials, education, and anything else that presents you favorably.

3. A visual of your office/personnel – A group photo in front of your office sign would be perfect.

4. Statistical information regarding your company – Closed sales, sales per agent, growth, whatever you are proud of, highlight it.

5. Pictures of houses you have sold – This is powerful. Put nine photos (and addresses) on each page and then include as many pages as you can. By the time the prospect has turned all those pages, they will know you can get the job done.

6. Copies of letters of praise – Few things are more powerful than a letter from a satisfied client expressing how great you are. You can never have too many of these in your pre-listing package.

7. Copies of award certificates – It doesn't matter if they are just for 'Agent of the Month' for your office (and not, in your mind, a big deal). If you earned it, include it.

8. Any newspaper or magazine stories in which you have been featured or quoted – There is something about being in print that enhances credibility.

9. A list of references – Be sure you have the permission of your references before including them.

10. A personal page – I have a page filled with pictures of my family. I want the sellers to feel confident and comfortable with me. Providing a more complete picture of who I am helps accomplish this.

11. A list of questions sellers should ask a prospective listing agent – See List # 37.

36

15 Steps To Getting
The Listing Every Time

Everyone in real estate knows (or should know) that listings are the key to success. Listings worked properly not only earn you a fee but they provide you with future buyer client opportunities as well as future seller opportunities. When you lose a listing you not only lose that chance but all the others down the line. Because of this you NEVER want to lose a listing. Here are 15 steps you should take to ensure you give yourself the best chance to get the listing.

1. Do your research beforehand – There is so much information available online that there is no excuse for you not knowing nearly everything you need to know before you even step in the door. Tax records will give you the specifics of the house, Zillow.com can offer an estimated price, and municipal records can tell you what the seller paid and what they owe. You may even be able to learn about the sellers through Facebook and LinkedIn.

2. Deliver your pre-listing marketing piece at least 24 hours prior to your appointment – Predispose the sellers to want to hire you even before you arrive by providing them with an awesome pre-listing package. See List #35 for more about the prelisting marketing piece.

3. Dress for success – This is a job interview. Dress professionally.

4. Be exactly on time - Arriving late will cause you to start the meeting with an apology. Not good. Arriving early may cause embarrassment for the sellers if they are not ready for you. Also not good. Plan to get there 10 minutes early, park your car around the corner, and pull into the driveway exactly on time.

5. Take control of the appointment from the beginning – Someone is going to lead the meeting. You want that someone to be you. Skillfully take charge by . . .

6. Ask to go to the kitchen table so you can talk a few minutes – Many agents start by asking to see the house. This is a mistake. You want to establish rapport and learn what the seller's goals are. The best way to do that is at the kitchen table. That's where friends usually sit. That's where you should sit too. What if they don't have a kitchen table? Use the dining room table.

7. Explain to them how you work – Lay out your process beginning with asking questions, seeing the house, reviewing your marketing plan, deciding on price, etc. Besides giving you control, this also lets the seller know what to expect which will cause them to relax.

8. Ask questions – The sellers have a problem; they own a house they no longer need. But they have another problem. Something has changed in their lives to cause them to move. If you understand what that issue is, you are on your way to better helping them.

9. Ask more questions – See List #38. You cannot ask too many questions.

10. Show genuine interest in their house – When it comes time to see the house, be genuinely interested in it. Take notes. To you it might be one of a dozen you will be in that week but for them it is their home. Show them respect by being acutely interested in their house.

11. Use visuals to demonstrate your marketing plan – People remember far more of what they see than what they hear. Don't tell them your office is #1, show them a list with your company at the top. Don't tell them you have sold 200 houses – give them a list of 200 addresses. Better yet, have pictures of the houses. Visuals make a powerful impression.

12. Write the description for their home that you will use in the MLS – Remember #1 of this list – do your research. You should be able to write an effective description from all you can learn even before you see the house. It won't be as complete since you had not seen the house yet (and you can tell the seller that) but you will be demonstrating initiative and setting yourself apart from any other agent they may be considering.

13. Show them the marketing brochure for their home – You should be able to take a photo of the house from the street beforehand. Use it to show the sellers one of the ways you will market their home.

14. Ask for the listing – Don't do a great presentation then not ask for the listing. You're a salesperson – they expect you to ask.

15. Follow up with a letter thanking them – They may not be ready to say 'yes' to you just yet. A letter thanking them for the chance to be their agent may seal the deal for you.

Matt Williams

37

12 Questions You Should Be Prepared To Answer on a Listing Presentation

A listing presentation is a job interview. Expect to be asked questions. Here are 12 you want to be sure you have answers for. (Note: I <u>want</u> to be asked these questions and I want any other agent the seller may be interviewing to be asked these questions, too. To see that happens, I include a page with these questions in my pre-listing package).

1. "How long have you sold real estate?"

2. "Is selling real estate your only job?"

3. "How many houses have you successfully marketed (listed) in the last three years?"

4. "What percentage of listings you take actually sell?"

5. "The houses that did not sell, why didn't they sell?"

6. "What percentage of the original list price do your listings sell for?"

7. "What is the average time it takes for you to sell your listings?"

8. "What percentage of your business involves working with sellers?"

9. "What specifically will you do to market my house?"

10. "Will you give me the names of your last 5 seller clients?"

11. "Do you intend to be away during the time of the listing?"

12. "If I am not happy with your effort or results, may I terminate the listing without condition?"

Key Takeaway

Sellers typically list with the agent they feel most confident about. The more confident you are the more likely the seller will choose you. Your confidence comes from being prepared. You may never be asked these questions, but if you are you don't want to stumble over your answers. Be prepared.

38

10 Questions You Must Ask Every Seller

The better you understand your seller's life situation the better you'll be able to provide the service they need. Too many agents barrel through the house within seconds of arriving on the listing presentation without ever stopping to ask what the seller is trying to accomplish. After establishing rapport, the most important thing an agent can do is get answers to these 10 questions.

1. Why are you selling? It is not simply because they decided to sell the house. Something else is going on in their life. Understand what that is and you are on the way to crafting a solution to their problem.

2. Why now – why not a year ago or a year from now? This helps clarify the 'why'.

3. Where are you moving? Will they need you to find them a new house or will you be referring them out of state? Understand as best you can what they are trying to accomplish.

4. What is there for you? This helps clarify the 'why'.

5. When do you need to be there? You are in a better position to counsel them if you understand their urgency.

6. What will it mean to you if you are not there by then? I think this is the most important question you can ask. What is the consequence of being unsuccessful?

7. As you think about selling your house what keeps you up at night? Knowing what they fear is the first step to showing how you can make it so those fearful situations never happen.

8. What is most important to you – getting the highest price, having an uncomplicated sale, or selling it promptly? It's not always the highest price. I once had a client who was dying of cancer. He wanted his wife to be resettled before he died. His first agent didn't know this and priced the house too high. I recommended a lower price, the house sold quickly, and his wife was in her new home before he died.

9. What does success look like to you? If you could script exactly what happens and when it happens what would it look like? Let them tell you what they want to happen. Listen carefully.

10. What do you expect from your real estate agent? Listen carefully to what they say. They are telling you what is important to them. Then, tailor your presentation to those needs.

Key Takeaway

Be sure to listen to the answers. They are giving you valuable information.

39

8 Likely Situations Every 'For Sale By Owner' (FSBO) Seller Needs To Know They May Face

The biggest challenge in working with for sale by owner sellers is getting them to realize what they don't know. Even if the FSBO rejects the idea that the exposure a real estate agent can offer (among other benefits) will net the seller more money, the FSBO will have a harder time dealing with certain real life situations. Here are 8 situations (in question form) you should discuss with any FSBO you are prospecting.

Each question begins, "What will you do, Mr. FSBO . . ."

1. **When the buyers say they love the house and then offer you $50,000 below your asking price?** – Are these skilled negotiators trying to take advantage of your lack of representation? Perhaps they are very capable buyers who are relying on erroneous information to make their offer?

2. **When they say they love the house, want to buy it, but need some time to sell their present home?** – How much time? Is the house on the market yet? What's the market like where they live now? Are they going to be reasonable in their asking price or do they have "the best house on the street" and expect to be paid handsomely?

3. **When they ask if they could be alone in the house for a while so they can "try it on for size"?** – Will the homeowner be comfortable leaving strangers alone in his house? Or will he inadvertently insult them (perhaps driving them away) by denying the request, thus implying they are not trustworthy?

4. **When they refuse to give you proof they can afford the house?** – And they are shocked that you would even ask such

a personal question. Or they say, "Money is no problem". Is it? How do you find out?

5. **When they tell you their house inspector found 25 items that need to be corrected including high levels of radon, evidence of asbestos, and an old buried oil tank you didn't even know was there?** – Is there proof? Is the proof legitimate or is the buyer a shark preying on naïve sellers?

6. **When they tell you they need a 6% seller's concession?** – Do you even know what a seller's concession is? Do you realize how this affects the mortgage and appraisal?

7. **When they tell you they are not going to use an attorney?** –How will your attorney communicate with the buyer? What if the buyer doesn't return calls?

8. **Finally, ask the seller what they will do if they get two or more buyers at the same time?** – How do they determine which is the better offer? How do they determine if either offer is legitimate? How do they accept one offer without alienating the other buyer so that if the first offer falls through, the seller can try to make a deal with the second buyer?

Key Takeaway

Selling a home is a complex and difficult undertaking. Most FSBOs have no idea what they are getting themselves into. Help them make the right decision by showing them what is involved.

Section 5

---◆---

Servicing The Listing

Matt Williams

40

10 Things Sellers Do To Mess Up Sales

Why would anybody do anything purposely to hurt their chances of selling their home? It doesn't make sense yet people do it all the time. One of the roles of a real estate agent is to protect the client from making poor choices. Before we can do that we need to recognize what some of those bad choices are. Here are 10 things sellers do that are contrary to their best interest and that you must do your best to protect them from.

1. **Price their house too high** – Whether it is due to ignorance, greed, or misplaced hope, the #1 reason a house doesn't sell is it is priced too high. Sellers who price their home wisely are far more likely to get the highest price for their homes than sellers who do not.

2. **They insist on complicated showing instructions** – I understand that sometimes there are pets that need tending to but the instructions that say 'Call the wife on her cell and leave a message. Then call the husband on his cell. If you don't reach him, call the neighbor" are not good for the seller. Anything that makes it difficult to show has the potential of keeping the buyer that would pay the highest price from seeing the home. The best instructions are 'Call-leave message-Go'.

3. **They limit the availability of showings** – "Sunday showings only", "No showings before noon", "Listing agent must accompany". Bad, Bad, Bad.

4. **They stay at the house during showings** – Buyers hate when the seller is present. They don't relax, they can't speak freely with their agent, and they are hesitant to linger and

really experience the house. Sellers should not be present during showings.

5. **They take the advice of well meaning but misinformed friends** – Sellers often put more faith in what their cousin (who has sold exactly one house in his life) says than in the agent who does this every day. Whether it is pricing, negotiating strategy, or marketing, everyone has a friend who is a real estate "expert".

6. **They don't make the house look the best it can** – The kitty litter box goes unemptied, there is a pile of boots in the kitchen, the beds aren't made, and on and on and on. You would never sell your car without washing, waxing, vacuuming, and scenting it. Your house requires the same treatment.

7. **They select the wrong realtor** – All real estate agents are not the same. Some are simply more effective than others. Yet many sellers do no research at all when they choose their agent.

8. **They think a quick offer means the house was priced too low** – If the house is priced properly it should get a quick offer. But many sellers decide to be stubborn when they get an offer in the first days on the market. Months later, long after the buyer has moved on to another house, the sellers grudgingly accept an offer thousands of dollars less.

9. **They act emotionally** – At its core selling a house is a business transaction yet many sellers cast aside logic and instead act emotionally. The reaction, in response to a low offer, "I'll burn the house down before I sell it to that guy" is an example of a seller acting with his heart and not his head.

10. **They treat their agent like she is the enemy** – When this happens the agent must bear some responsibility for having not earned the trust and respect of the seller. That said, many sellers hurt themselves by being suspicious from the start and not showing confidence in their agent.

41

5 Things Sellers Have Full Control Over That Affect The Sale of Their House

Many sellers feel a sense of helplessness when they sell. They think they have little to no control over the outcome and that their fate is out of their hands. However, sellers do have significant influence over the sale of their home. In fact, they have compete control over these fives aspects to selling a home. Make your sellers understand their responsibility and you will help them be more successful.

1. The agent they choose to represent them – All agents and all companies are not the same. Some agents do a better job than others. The seller that does their research and makes a wise choice has taken a big step towards being successful.

2. The price they list the house for – Besides selecting the right agent, pricing the house properly is the most important thing a seller can do.

3. The condition of the house when it is shown – Well-presented homes sell faster and for more money than houses that are dirty and unattractive. It's that simple. Sellers who prepare their home properly increase the likelihood of a sale.

4. The availability for showings – Sellers who refuse showings or make it difficult to arrange showings limit their chance for a sale.

5. Their response to offers – Nobody says a seller needs to be happy with a low offer but years of negotiating has taught me it doesn't matter where the parties begin, but instead, where they finish that matters. Even if the offer is low, don't allow your sellers to let it get personal. Instead, work to bring the parties together.

Matt Williams

42

10 Tips For Taking Great Photos

My long-time mentor Floyd Wickman is fond of saying "A picture is worth a thousand bucks". He's right. Photos are critically important in marketing a house. Here are 10 tips for taking photos that sell houses.

1. Use a good camera with a wide-angle lens – You don't have to spend a lot - $200-$300 will get you a camera that will do the trick.

2. Remove distractions from the point of view – Move the garbage cans out of sight, have the owner get their car out of the way, and get the toys off the lawn. You want nothing to distract from the house/yard.

3. Be certain the light is behind you – This may mean you need to make two trips (one in the morning, the other in the afternoon) but having the light right is critical when taking outside photos.

4. Take the photo from an angle to show depth – Straight on shots look two-dimensional. Shoot the house from an angle. Not only will this add depth to your photo, it allows you to show more of the house.

5. Don't take portrait orientation cell phone pictures – I hesitate to say never use a smartphone camera because many are good. But never, never, NEVER take photos in the portrait orientation. They are not formatted properly for display on the many real estate websites.

6. Try to shoot down on the subject – use a ladder or truck – Though difficult to do, if you can shoot down slightly on the house you add a dimension of depth that makes many homes more attractive. A selfie-stick can help.

7. Make certain the subject of the photo constitutes ¾ of the image – Never use a photo that cuts off the house.

8. Don't be afraid to include photos of something besides the house – Your marketing photos can include anything that adds to the enjoyment of the viewer. Gardens, views, impressive trees, ponds, street scenes, and more can all work to encourage a viewer to investigate further. Use your imagination.

9. Experiment with flash – Flash sometime creates a washed out look. Other times it is better than natural light. Take your photos using both and use the one that's better.

10. If something changes during the time you have the house listed – for example, flowers bloom – take new photos – Don't be the agent with photos of a snow-covered lawn in June. Not only does this scream 'lazy agent', it also tells buyers the house has been on the market a long time. Not good.

Key Takeaway

The importance of having great photos in marketing a property cannot be overemphasized. You should be able to do this yourself, but, if you simply cannot take good pictures, hire a professional photographer. There is no excuse for poor photos.

43

9 Tips For Writing Great Listing Descriptions

The words that appear in your advertisements and MLS descriptions very often will determine whether a buyer will decide to take a look at the listing. Consequently the words you use are very important to the success of the sale. Here are 9 tips for writing descriptions that make buyers want to see your listing.

1. **Give this task the time and attention it deserves** – Many agents look at this as a nuisance and rush through the process as quickly as possible. Don't do this. Close the door to your office, fix yourself a cup of tea, and settle in for an endeavor that should not be rushed.

2. **Make a list of every feature of the house, property, and location** – Three bedrooms, 1 ½ baths, family room, basketball hoop, laundry, distance to the train station, new roof, hardwood floors, new windows, etc. Write down everything.

3. **Decide on the features that will likely be important to a potential buyer** – Put a star next to each.

4. **Have handy a list of descriptive words** – Some examples can be found on List # 44.

5. **Write a story using words of feeling that takes the reader on a journey through the house** – Be certain to have some sense of order to your tour. Don't write about the kitchen and then write about the backyard and then write about the bathroom in the master bath. Give the reader the opportunity to imagine what it is you are describing.

6. **Don't use abbreviations unless absolutely necessary** - And never, never, never use abbreviations that are only understood by real estate people like DE Bath, WIC, etc.

7. Separate individual room or area descriptions with a hyphen - This will minimize the appearance of run-on sentences and make it easier for your reader to read, which will increase the likelihood that they will read the whole thing.

8. Lead the story with a descriptive of that feature you feel is most likely to influence the purchaser's decision – And stay away from overused real estate ad phrases (see List # 45).

9. When you're finished give your copy to someone you trust to be honest with you and ask them what they think – Be sure your description is clear, accurate, and enticing.

#44

56 Great Adjectives To Use In Your Ads And Listing Descriptions

When a buyer looks over a listing on the Internet or a listing sent to them by their agent, their decision to see it or not (assuming it meets the buyer's basic needs) depends largely on the photos and the description in the listing. If the description excites the buyer, they make the appointment to see it. If the description is boring, they may not. Here are 56 great adjectives that can move buyers to want to see your listing.

Gorgeous
Affordable
Private
Rare
Enchanting
Dramatic
Impeccable
Magnificent
Impressive
Warm
Classic
Relaxing
Showplace
Gracious
Gleaming
Spacious
Antique
Expansive
Colorful
Sun filled
Quiet
Meticulous
Tree lined
Soaring

Marvelous
Rich
Historic
Sumptuous
Bright
Sunny
Oversized
Delightful
Intimate
Formal
Distinctive
Traditional
Soothing
Fabulous
Impressive
Stunning
Desirable
Splendid
Exquisite
Tremendous
Grandiose
Stately
Majestic
Plush
Spotless
Memorable
Remarkable
Captivating
Flawless
Pleasant
Extraordinary
Sophisticated

45

9 Advertising Phrases That Probably Should Be Retired Permanently

It's time we said goodbye to these ineffective and sometimes insulting phrases that have too long been part of real estate advertising.

1. **"Priced to sell"** – Empty words that don't mean anything. The price speaks for itself. It doesn't need a translator.

2. **"Won't last"** – Are we talking about the house or the listing? It's funny when you see this in a listing description for a house that has been on the market more than a year.

3. **"Owner says sell"** – A cousin to #1 above. Empty words.

4. **"Must see"** – This means nothing to a buyer. Besides, who buys a house without seeing it?

5. **"To show it is to sell it"** – If this is true then no one must be showing it. Or else why is it still on the market?

6. **"Priced below market"** – This borders on false advertising. If it were priced below market, somebody would've already bought it.

7. **"Motivated seller"** – If the seller is especially motivated he should be lowering his price rather than announcing he's motivated.

8. **"Freshly painted"** –When I see this phrase it reminds me of the old phrase, "Let's put lipstick on this pig". That's not a good association.

9. **"Amazing opportunity"** – Really! 'Amazing' can mean many things – not all of them are good.

46

26 Things You Should Do Within 24 Hours Of Taking a Listing

It has been said a task well begun is a task half completed. Get off to a great start by making sure all these steps are taken.

1. Obtain and verify accurate methods of contacting the sellers including email, home phone, and mobile phone – Ask how they prefer you communicate with them.

2. Research tax records to verify accurate information is available to prospective buyers and their agents – The house seems to have 4 bedrooms but the tax record says it has 3. Now, not three months from now, is when you should straighten out the discrepancy.

3. Analyze current tax assessment to ensure it's accurate – Assessors sometimes make mistakes. Sometimes those mistakes discourage potential buyers from seeing the house. Make certain the tax assessment is correct.

4. Review with seller complete selling process – Let them know what the steps of the sale are.

5. Conduct an inspection of the house to suggest constructive changes that will make the house more appealing thus yielding the greatest possible price – Pretend you are a buyer. Make a list of everything that can be improved.

6. Provide the homeowner with instructions how they are to reach you.

7. **Get the name and contact information for the seller's attorney or title company** – If they don't know yet it is fine. There's plenty of time.

8. **Collect copies of tax bills** – Check them for accuracy.

9. **Determine what, if any, environmental issues affect the property and must be disclosed** – Things like floodplain, wetlands, Superfund sites, etc.

10. **Collect copies of all certificates of occupancy and compliance** – Finding out 5 days before closing that the addition never got a C/O can kill a deal. Make sure everything is legal from the get-go.

11. **Determine if there is a buried oil tank** – If the seller says there is not, go look for signs of one anyway. They may not be aware there is one.

12. **If tank has been removed or decommissioned, make copies of all paperwork** – You are going to need them eventually. It's best to get them now.

13. **Take quality photos to highlight the home's special features** – See List # 42.

14. **Collect two years of heating and electric bills** – Not every buyer wants to see them but those that do will appreciate you being able to provide them promptly.

15. **Review with seller how to prepare the house for showing.**

16. **Measure room sizes for marketing purposes** – The more information you can put in your listing description the more time potential buyers will spend investigating the listing.

17. **Collect two sets of keys** – One for the lockbox and the other is a spare set to be kept in your office.

18. Compile a list of homeowner improvements with dates – Be certain you have receipts to verify the dates. Otherwise you may find yourself in court defending a misrepresentation. If you can't prove it, don't say it.

19. Announce the listing to your office colleagues through email and voicemail – Deals typically go better when working with an agent in your own office. Give them a heads up when there is new inventory.

20. Enter the listing in the appropriate multiple listing services.

21. Print copies of the MLS listing and forward to seller for their review for accuracy – Have them sign off that the information in the listing is correct and keep a copy in your file.

22. If needed, arrange for shoe covers to be placed in foyer – You can buy 100 for about $15 at Amazon.com.

24. Confirm with seller how they want to be contacted when appointments are scheduled – With technology allowing contact by phone, email, and text, you want to be sure the sellers are contacted in the medium that will get to them promptly.

25. Place lawn sign on property – Dollar for dollar the lawn sign remains the real estate agent's best advertising tool.

26. Prepare full-color brochure – I doubt having a brochure on display has ever convinced a buyer to buy a particular house but an attractive marketing piece can lend an air of quality to the house. Also, sellers love (and expect) them. You may even impress a buyer who's not thrilled with the agent who is showing them houses now.

Matt Williams

47

9 Simple Things a Real Estate Agent Can Do To Help Make a Listing More Salable

It doesn't typically fall under the responsibility of the real estate agent to make improvements to a property for the seller. That said, going the extra mile for your client can create great dividends in customer satisfaction (and future referrals) and it may make your job selling the house easier. With a simple toolkit and less than $100 you may be able to improve your product so it sells weeks earlier and for more money. Here are some things you can do.

(Note: Before doing anything you want to have the seller's permission. Usually the sellers will take care of these things themselves, but sometimes they have already vacated the home or they are elderly and incapable of doing the work.)

1. **Replace the shabby welcome mat with a new one** – First impressions matter. For a few bucks you can switch out the ratty old mat with a more attractive one.

2. **Clean up reasonable messes on the front yard** – 30 minutes with a rake and a garbage can mean the difference between making a place look homey instead of a dump.

3. **Lubricate squeaky hinges** – A squirt of WD-40 will do the trick on door and cabinet hinges.

4. **Move clutter items into closets or the basement** – Relocate nonessential items to the corners of the basement. By the time the buyer sees them they likely will have already made the decision to buy or pass on the house.

5. **Donate some potted plants to dress up the front stoop** – Not only do they make the house look nicer, once the deal is

done you can move them onto your next listing or your own home.

6. **If a wall is missing a piece of artwork, let the sellers borrow some from you** - Sellers I've done this for have always been grateful.

7. **Move the garbage cans around to the back of the house** – If the garbage cans are out in the front of the house they are the first thing the potential buyer notices. You don't want that.

8. **Reorganize existing furniture to better stage the property** – The way people live is not necessarily the way they sell. The sofa may be very convenient in the center of the family room but if it makes for an awkward traffic flow, it's better to reposition it while the house is on the market. Remember, everyone does not have the ability to see past what is to what it could be.

9. **Paint around the front door**– Peeling paint is a turn off. Having it the first thing you see is a major mistake.

<u>Key Takeaway</u>

There are so many things that we don't control in the process of selling a house that we need to control the things we can. You can argue that spiffing up a property is not your job, and you'd be correct, but the owner is not the only one in the transaction with a financial interest; the real estate agent has a financial interest too. If you can invest an hour and a few dollars making your listing more desirable, it might be the difference between you making a sale (and earning a commission) and not making a sale.

48

6 Things To Report To Your Sellers Each Week

Successful sellers are successful because they make good decisions. Good decisions come from having good information. The real estate agent must be the source of that information. Get in the habit of communicating with your sellers on a regular basis and you will have more sellers making good decisions and you will close more sales. Here's what your sellers need to know.

1. **The feedback for recent showings** – Let them know what other agents and their buyers are saying about price, condition, and overall salability.

2. **Any comparable new listings** – Is there new competition? How does it compare to their house?

3. **The changed status of any comparable listings** – Have any of the other comparable homes lowered their price, accepted an offer, expired?

4. **Analytic data from the MLS or other Internet advertising sites** – How many views is your listing getting?

5. **Your marketing efforts that week** – Did you host an open house, run an ad, send out a marketing piece to your real state database? Tell the seller what you are doing for them.

6. **Any external factors that may affect their sale** – Has a local employer announced they are expanding or closing? Have interest rates increased or fallen? Is there anything else the seller should know that affects demand?

Matt Williams

12 Steps To Getting a Price Reduction

Helping sellers make right decisions is one of the great responsibilities of the real estate agent. The truth is people don't always do what they should. That's why the real estate agent has to help them. One of the most common mistakes sellers make is pricing their house too high. For the seller to be successful, it is often necessary to show them the error of their ways and lower the price. Here are 12 steps you should take to get a price reduction.

1. **Make certain the problem is price and not your lack of marketing** – Have you done everything you can to expose the house to potential buyers?

2. **Be certain to have communicated regularly with your client** – Few things upset a seller more than listing the property with an agent, not hearing from her for a month, and then getting a phone call telling them they have to lower the price. Even if you have nothing to say, call them every week and let them know they are still on your radar.

3. **Share information with them regularly** – New listings of comparable homes, new closings, price reductions – send off a quick email with this information with a note that says FYI. Keep them informed.

4. **Gather feedback to present to the owner** – The house hasn't been shown, you say, and there is no feedback? Wrong. You <u>do</u> have feedback – the real estate community and the buying public have both determined the price is too high - which is why no one has come see the house. If you do have feedback from agents, share it with the seller.

5. **Call the seller and ask when they'll have 15 minutes of uninterrupted time that you can talk** – Be ready to talk immediately as they will often say "Now is good".

6. **Be sure you know before you call what price you need to be at** – You will get one shot to do this right. Don't let your knees buckle and tell them something between their current price and the right price.

7. **Let them down slowly** – They probably already know why you're calling. Use a dialogue like this, "Thanks for taking the time to talk to me. I never enjoy making these calls but they are necessary. Let me take a minute and review what has happened with your listing so far."

8. **Don't leave anything out** – Recap your advertisements, promotions, open houses, broker open houses, web activity, feedback, etc. – tell them everything you have done to attract attention to the house.

9. **Conclude by saying it is unfortunate but the market has clearly rejected your price** – Explain that a price improvement will be necessary to make possible a sale.

10. **Ask them if they would like to know what the price should be** - If they say yes, tell them. If they don't want to know, tell them anyway.

11. **Explain the consequences of being overpriced** – Remember when you asked all those questions on the listing presentation? One was, "What happens if you don't sell by the time you need to?" Now is the time to remind them.

12. **Close for the price reduction** – Close again (and again), if necessary.

Section 6

---◆---

Open Houses

Matt Williams

50

12 Ways an Agent Can
Make Money at an Open House

Many agents think open houses are a waste of time. If that's what they truly believe, they are right – it is a self-fulfilling prophecy. But hundreds of agents happily put their directional signs out every Sunday. A fundamental building block of a successful real estate career is initiating new relationships with buyers and sellers. Every Sunday afternoon current buyers and future sellers can be found visiting open houses and meeting real estate agents. Here are a dozen ways an agent can earn money from an open house.

1. **Sell the house to a visitor** – "We love it. We'll take it." This doesn't happen all the time but it does happen often.

2. **List the house of a visitor** – They may not think much of the house but they did think highly of you and they ask for you to list their home.

3. **List the house of a neighbor you meet** – You sent a letter inviting the neighbor to the open house. They liked the way you reached out to them.

4. **Meet a buyer by way of one of the guests** – "This house isn't right for me but my friend is looking, too. I think she'll love it. Can I have her call you?"

5. **Meet a neighbor who has a child/friend who wants to buy** – "We got your letter and came to talk with you. Our son and daughter in law are moving here from Portland and . . . ".

6. **Meet a neighbor who has a child/friend who wants to sell** – "We got your letter. Our daughter has to sell her house. We like that you sent this letter. Can you help our daughter?"

7. **Refer a neighbor who is relocating** – "We got your letter. I am only renting this house and I am moving to _____. Do you have any office's there?"

8. **Attract the attention of a seller via your ad** – "We were busy on Sunday and could not come to your open house. We live 2 blocks over. How's the market?"

9. **Attract the attention of a buyer via your ad** – "We were busy on Sunday and could not come to the open house. Can you show it to us during the week?"

10. **List the home of someone looking for an agent** – "How do we like the house? Oh, we're not interested in the house. So why did we come? We're looking for an agent to sell our home and we wanted to see how you worked."

11. **Meeting someone results in an out-of-area referral** – "I'm not quite ready to buy as I just inherited a house in _____ and I need to sell that house first. Do you have an office in _____?"

12. **Sell another house to a buyer** – "This house isn't for us. Would you help us find another one?"

51

12 Steps To Open House Success

Open houses can be a great way to meet new buyer and seller prospects. Like anything else, there is a right way and a wrong way to do open houses. Here are 12 things you can do to make your open houses more successful for you.

1. **Start with the right attitude** – Open houses should be seen as a great opportunity to meet new prospects, not an obligation.

2. **Have the right goals** – There are four: 1. Present the house to as many potential buyers as positively as possible, 2. Capture the names and contact information for each visitor, 3. Have the visitors feel positively about you, and 4. Obtain permission to contact them again.

3. **Approach doing open houses as you would a job interview** – Because that's exactly what it is. Dress properly, be prepared, be focused, and be your best with every visitor you meet.

4. **Select the right house** – It should be a desirable property with broad appeal in an easily accessible location. It should also be priced so that it is a 'move up' home, affording you listing as well as selling opportunities.

5. **Invite the neighbors** – Most people don't know a real estate agent so when you invite neighbors you are opening the door to become their real estate agent when the time comes . . . which might be very soon.

6. **Be prepared** – Arrive early, set up lots of directional signs, be aware of similar properties that may be suitable for your visitors, have your marketing materials displayed attractively, and know your product.

7. **Create a positive energy atmosphere** – You want people to linger so you have a greater opportunity to establish a relationship. Don't go overboard but to try to create a fun environment.

8. **Offer a giveaway** – A free mortgage preapproval certificate, a coupon worth $500 off on their closing fees, or a certificate for a free market analysis may help establish a new relationship with a visitor.

9. **Don't smother your visitors** – The average open house visitor spends less than 10 minutes in the house. That's not enough time for you to establish a lasting relationship but is enough time to destroy a relationship irreparably. Remember your goal (see #2 above).

10. **Leave your visitors feeling positive about you** – You want them to feel good about their experience with you, even if the house is not for them.

11. **Add your visitor's names to your database** – You will want to invite them to future open houses, advise them of any price changes to your open house listing, and let them know of any new inventory that may meet their needs. Remember, it's about relationship.

12. **Follow up** – A simple phone call to ask for feedback for the seller may open up an opportunity for discussion that will lead to another appointment.

52

5 Misguided Reasons For Doing Open Houses

Open houses can be an integral part of many agents' business plans.
Done for the right reasons open houses can yield great dividends.
Too many agents however do open houses for the wrong reasons.
Here are 5 of those reasons:

1. **The seller insisted the agent do an open house** – The house may be overpriced, in poor condition, and in a remote location - in other words, a poor house to hold open. Do open houses on your terms, not because the seller told you to.

2. **The agent is about to lose the listing and wants to show the sellers they are doing something** – If you are doing the open house because it is part of your business plan, that's good. But if you're just doing it for show you are wasting your time and misleading your seller.

3. **There is no showing activity and the agent doesn't know what else to do** – If you are doing your job marketing the property and still no one comes, you need to lower the price.

4. **Their manager is making them do an open house** – Open houses are a great way to meet potential clients but if the agent is being dragged into doing them kicking and screaming by his manager he would probably be better off not doing it at all. Better to keep that bad attitude out of sight than to put it out on display.

5. **One of the other agents in the office asked them** – Real estate offices are full of persuasive people. Don't let yourself be persuaded into hosting a bad open house (see the list on the next page) for one of your persuasive colleagues..

Matt Williams

10 Factors That Contribute To Failed Open Houses

One of the reasons agents hate open houses is their experience has been negative. A big part of that has to do with holding the wrong house open. You are trying to create relationships and you need to do everything you can to encourage people to come and stay at your open house. Here is a list of things that work against that.

1. The house is a mess - Visitors can't get out of there fast enough when a house is messy.

2. The house is located in a remote location - Plan on being alone if your open house is not in an area that people are in.

3. The owners insist on staying - Do you want to experience the longest three hours of your life? Let the owners stay during an open house. Not only is this bad for you, but visitors who know the owner is there usually don't stay long.

4. The house does not have broad appeal - You want to host at a house everyone wants to see. Stay clear of the houses that only a small segment of the market would be interested in.

5. Access to the house is limited - You won't have many visitors if there's no place for them to park or the busy street makes it impractical for them to stop.

6. The house is unattractive from the street - If the house is ugly people don't stop.

7. The house is significantly overpriced - Buyers aren't stupid and they don't visit houses that are priced so incorrectly as to be insulting. It's not a good reflection on you either.

8. The area around the house is substandard - The neighborhood matters and even if this house is beautiful, if the neighborhood is not, many potential visitors won't stop.

9. The house is not visible from the road – Some (most) open house visitors simply will not venture down the driveway that they don't know where it leads.

10. There is something wrong with the house you need to apologize for to every visitor - If the roof has a tarp on it, the basement is flooded, or there is anything else "the seller plans on fixing", don't do the open house until those things are done.

12 Productive Things You Can Do At An Open House That No One Comes To

Hey it happens. You do everything you are supposed to do to promote your open house but no one comes. So what do you do – watch television? Wander through the house? Let your balloons go and watch them drift off into outer space? You can do those things but you can also make productive use of that time if you want. Here are 12 things you can do to advance your business at an open house where nobody comes.

1. **Plan your upcoming week/month** - Use this time to plan better use of the upcoming week/month.

2. **Organize your email inbox** - Who has time to delete all those junk emails? You do, now, if no one comes to your open house.

3. **Call people on your sphere of influence list** - Tell them you're at an open house. Tell them you are thinking of them. See where the conversation goes.

4. **Organize your purse/briefcase** - You might find a lead you have forgotten. At the very least you will be more organized.

5. **Read one of the books from List #27-** You are awake, alert, and have time. It's a great opportunity to learn from other's writings.

6. **Listen to a downloaded podcast** - Maybe you're not a reader. No problem, you can learn from one of thousands of podcasts you can download for free.

7. **Call one of the neighbors you sent an invitation to** - Hopefully you sent letters to the neighbors inviting them to

your open house. Call them and invite them again. It may be just the nudge they need to come visit and begin a relationship with you.

8. **Make follow-up phone calls** - There are always follow-up calls to make. Sunday afternoon is a great time to find people at home, relaxed, and with time to talk with you.

9. **Practice your listing presentation** - Use the camera on your smart phone to record yourself doing your listing presentation and learn where there are areas you can improve.

10. **Just think** - One downside of our connected culture is that we rarely have time to just think. We are always connected to others via our phone. That's unfortunate as some of our best ideas come out of quiet time. Shut off your phone for 30 minutes and just think of whatever comes to mind.

11. **Prepare a mailing** - Rather than take family time later, use this time to put those labels and stamps on your postcards.

12. **Call FSBOs nearby** - Invite them to your open house so they can see the competition. You never know where it may lead. The worst that can happen is nothing but the best that could happen is they come and you begin a relationship with them.

Key Takeaway

A 'no-visitor' open house is a waste of time only if you make it a waste of time. It is your choice.

Section 7

Working With Buyers

Matt Williams

10 Things Buyers Do To Mess Up Sales

Buyers are easily forgiven for acting in ways inconsistent with their best interest simply because most of them are inexperienced. That's why the real estate agent has to be skilled in protecting them from themselves. Here are 10 things buyers do that they need to be protected from.

1. **They rely on the advice of well meaning but misinformed friends and family** – These people mean well but their misguided counsel regarding value, negotiation strategy, and more often keep buyers from getting the home they should have.

2. **They begin the process without a clear idea of what it is they want to buy** – How will they know the right house if they don't know specifically what the right house is? The more clearly they can define what they want, the more likely they will get it. Don't let your buyers be vague.

3. **They don't arrange their financing before starting to look** – Would you ever go to the grocery store, load your cart, get on the checkout line and then look to see how much money you had on you? Of course not. But buyers do this all the time. First they should learn what their budget will allow. Then go look.

4. **They insist on looking at houses they cannot possibly afford** – Then, when they see the relatively modest houses they can afford, they are unhappy.

4. **They want to buy the 'Frankenhouse'** – You show them ten houses and ask which they like best. Their answer, "Well we like the kitchen at the first house, the yard at the third house,

the fireplace at the fifth house, etc". The house they just described is like Frankenstein – it's made up of parts of other houses. That house doesn't exist.

6. **They let their emotions get in the way** – It's understandable that there may be emotion involved with the purchase of a house, but you cannot let emotions rule. At its core, buying (or selling) a house is a business transaction. As with any business transaction it is best to be pragmatic and not emotional.

7. **They moved too slowly** – You snooze, you lose. Some markets move more briskly than others but no matter what market you are in, if the buyer has the chance to see or buy a house that may be perfect for them, waiting is not going to help. Someone else may swoop in and buy it or create a multiple offer situation causing the buyer to pay more. Buyers should move quickly.

8. **They don't educate themselves about radon, sump pumps, etc.** – Some issues rightly are deal killers. Unstable foundations and oil spills in the yard for example. But many buyers disqualify a house because the radon reading came in a little high, or more incredibly, because there is a radon mitigation system in the house. A little knowledge is dangerous. They know radon is troublesome but that's all they know. It is what they don't know that causes them to make poor decisions.

9. **They don't educate themselves about market value** – A successful outcome comes from making good decisions and good decisions come from having good data. Yet many buyers make offers based on what their friend did 5 years ago.

10. **They don't remain loyal to one agent** – Loyalty must be earned. The client owes the agent nothing. But once the agent has demonstrated their competence and commitment to the buyer's well being, looking at houses with multiple agents only serves to drive the agent who was best able to serve them away.

56

17 Questions You Must Ask Every Buyer

The fundamental job of real estate agents is not just to sell houses, but solve problems. One problem for buyers is they need a house and don't have one. But there is always something more. Something else is going on in their lives (family growing, new job, etc.) that prompted the search for a new home. The professional real estate agent seeks to understand what is going on in the buyer's life, i.e. understanding their needs, so she can better advise them. The way you uncover needs is by asking questions. Here are 17 questions you need to ask every buyer.

1. **What are you looking to do?** This is a good icebreaker. Asked in a friendly way the buyers will relax and provide a great deal of useful information.

2. **If you were writing a story of your home search, what would be a happy ending?** Stephen Covey, the author of *The Seven Habits of Highly Successful People*, says begin with the end in mind. Listen carefully to what they tell you a happy outcome is. That's what you're working towards.

3. **Are you preapproved for your mortgage?** If they are not, put them in touch was a good mortgage professional.

4. **Do you presently own a house?** You want to know the answer to this question for two reasons: 1. Is there a listing opportunity, and 2. Does something else have to happen before they can buy, i.e. sell another house.

5. **Do you have to sell it in order to buy your new home?** Oftentimes the answer is "no". But just because they can buy without selling it doesn't mean they will. That's why you have to ask the next question.

6. **Are you willing to own two homes?** Two homes means two tax bills, two utility bills, and maybe two mortgage payments, not to mention upkeep of two homes.

7. **Is it on the market/what is the status?** You need to understand what has to happen before they are able to buy.

8. **Do you have a lease?** If so, when is it up? Can you be let out of it?

9. **Where is it you commute to work?**

10. **How long a commute is the most you would accept?** Rather than asking, "Where do you want to live?", ask this question instead. The buyer may not be familiar with your entire market and you may be able to introduce them to an area they didn't know even existed.

11. **Describe the most important features your new home must have?** This is the fun part for them. Encourage them and write down everything they say. Be sure to ask the next question though.

12. **If you had to compromise on three of those features, which three could you live without?** The problem with the exhaustive list of 'wants' is that each additional want makes for a smaller selection. For example, if a buyer says they want a three-bedroom two-bath Cape, you will find more of them available than you will a three-bedroom, two bath Cape with a two-car garage, brick fireplace, in-ground pool, and first-floor master bedroom. After narrowing your selection with the question of their wants, this question expands their selection.

13. **When would you like to be in your new home?** Ideally you are looking for someone who has a very specific timeframe. Buyers who say, "We don't have a timetable. Whenever we find the right house is okay with us" often are not motivated. You want to work with motivated buyers.

14. Why that date? Listen carefully to the answer. It will be tied directly to the non-real estate problem I referenced earlier.

15. What happens if you are not in your new home by that day? This is the most important question of all and one the vast majority of realtors do not ask. You want to understand the consequence of not meeting that deadline. If there is no consequence the deadline has no meaning. But if there is a consequence you have a motivated buyer and someone worthy of your time.

16. Are you working with any other brokers? Better you find out upfront than farther down the road. If you are okay with them working with others, fine. But if you're not this will be the time to explain why you are not.

17. What are you looking for from me? The second most important question real estate agents rarely ask. Give them the opportunity to tell you what they want from you. Don't assume. Listen to what they say and then give them what they want. That's how you create loyal clients.

Matt Williams

57

7 Things Buyers Should Not Do When Getting A Mortgage

So the buyer hands you a preapproval letter. All is good, right? Well, maybe. The old saying, "Many a slip between cup and lip" certainly applies in the mortgage approval process. Here are 7 bits of advice you should share with your buyers no matter where they are in the mortgage process.

1. **Don't give the mortgage officer a whitewashed picture of your financial situation** – In other words, tell the truth. They are going to find out about that student loan you fell behind on, the alimony you're obligated to pay, or that other house you own but thought didn't matter.

2. **Don't leave the money for the down payment or closing costs in the stock market** - One bad day on Wall Street could leave you short of the funds to close.

3. **Don't make large deposits into your bank accounts that cannot be sourced** – If a deposit can't be sourced, lenders assume it is a loan, which may change everything.

4. **Don't miss any payments on any existing debt** – Even the smallest late payment will be a hot button for an underwriter and may cause them to reject the loan.

5. **Don't take on additional debt without first clearing it with your mortgage officer** – Any new debt (like a car payment) may throw off your ratios.

6. **Don't overdraw your checking account . . . even if you have overdraft protection** – Underwriters view this as a sign of financial mismanagement.

7. Don't take out any new credit cards or make new purchases – Even if you don't use the credit card and there is a balance of zero, the new credit line may lower your credit score.

58

8 Things Buyers Can Do To Improve The Odds Of Getting The House They Want

In a robust market there is often competition for good listings. A new house comes on the market and a dozen potential buyers rush to it. Multiple offers are submitted. Many buyers feel helpless but there are things they can do to influence the sellers in their favor. Here are 8.

1. Provide proof that your financing is already in place – The more secure the financing the more attractive the buyer is to the seller. Cash is best. Next is a mortgage commitment from a reputable lender. Worse is a simple pre-approval. Worst is nothing at all.

2. Offer to close at the convenience of the seller – Depending on the seller's situation, by being flexible with the closing date, your offer may be preferred over a higher offer that requires the seller to be out of the house in 30 days.

3. Offer to let them leave behind any furniture or unwanted personal property – This one is especially valuable when buying a home offered by an estate but it can also be the difference for sellers who are dealing with overwhelming issues not related to the sale of their home.

4. Have the buyer write a letter telling the seller how much they like their home – Personalizing the buyers by sharing the details of their family, life situation, and reasons they like the house may tip the scales in their favor.

5. Waive the engineering inspection – If your buyer is satisfied the house is in good condition they may gain an advantage by not making the deal contingent on an inspection. Be careful with this however. Suggesting the buyer not do an inspection may make you liable should a problem arise later. Be sure to have the buyer sign off formally that they are doing this with full knowledge of the risks.

6. Agree to accommodate the seller if a post occupancy is required – Closing quick and letting the seller rent back until they are ready to move may give your buyer an advantage.

7. Offer to place a large down payment in escrow – If the buyer has the resources, agreeing to a down payment in an amount greater than the customary 5%-10% may catch the seller's attention and make the difference.

8. Make an aggressive offer immediately – The buyer that wants a particular house shouldn't be shy about making an above asking price offer right from the start. While they may think you've lost your mind when you recommend starting at $10,000 over asking price, if you've done your homework and are secure that the house is worth it, you may be able to shut out the competition by making a very aggressive offer.

59

8 Ways To Get More Of
Your Buyer's Offers Accepted

The process of buying a home is a journey. Sometimes the road is smooth and easily traveled while other times it is rocky and treacherous. As the agent, your responsibility is to guide your client safely throughout this journey. One way is to control as much as you can. Nowhere is this more important than when presenting an offer. Your attitude, tone, and counsel in dealing with both your buyer client and the co-broke client may mean the difference between your client getting the house or not getting the house. Here are 8 things you must do every time you present an offer.

1. **In your mind commit to a win-win situation** - This simple act will enable you to better visualize areas of agreement and solutions to potential problems.

2. **Get a complete offer in writing** - Depending on your local custom the offer may or may not be signed. That's not important. What is important is that the complete offer is written and confirmed to be accurate by your buyer client.

3. **Have a hard copy of the preapproval letter** – And read it. Then verify it. Some 'pre approvals' are worthless.

4. **Call the other agent before you email them the offer** - Tell her you have good news – your buyer is interested in buying her listing. Even if it is a low offer begin by saying "I have good news . . ."

5. **Don't use the expression "my buyers". Instead, use their names** - When we use terms like "my buyers" and "your sellers" we are acting in an adversarial manner. If our goal is

to find agreement doesn't it make sense to work on taking down walls instead of building them?

6. **Tell the list agent about the buyers** – Many sellers prefer to sell – even if it is a lower price – to people they like. Let the seller know about the buyers - where they're coming from, what their interests are, why they like the house.

7. **No matter if the offer is full price or half-price, be upbeat and enthusiastic** - Many a deal was created and sustained on the strength of the agent's enthusiasm. If you're fortunate to work with another enthusiastic agent, that's great, but if the seller's agent is more of a drag, you'll have to redouble your enthusiastic effort. Remember, it's not where people start the negotiation but where they finish that matters.

8. **Always keep your eye on the goal – an agreement** - Ignore distractions such as assumptions, negative comments, etc.

60

7 Reasons Your Buyer Should Go Into a House They Reject From The Street

It happens often. You make an appointment to show a house but when you pull up to the curb the buyer says "No way" and they tell you to not even bother going in. Should you do what they say? No. Nearly every real estate agent has a story about selling a house the buyers initially refused to go in. You're not serving your client by letting them leave. Here are seven reasons/dialogs you can use to get your buyers out of the car and into the house.

1. **"It is a courtesy – the seller expects us"** – The seller reorganized their day around our visit. It's the polite thing to do.

2. **"You may not like this house but there may be something inside you have never seen before that you do like that you'll want in whatever house you buy."**

3. **Every real estate agent has a story of a buyer buying the house they initially refused to go into** – "What a shame if you missed this home".

4. **"You may feel differently when you see the inside"** – Sometimes you can judge a book by its cover, other times you can't.

5. **"This may help you understand the market value better once we know how much this house sells for"** – It's a chance to get more data and data is good when making decisions.

6. **"Would you please humor me. It's kind of an embarrassment to me to make the appointment and not go in."**

7. "We're here. It'll take five minutes". -What a shame if it was a house the buyer would have liked and you didn't see it even though you were right in front of it.

Section 8

————•————

Learning Along The Way

Matt Williams

61

24 Things I Wish I Knew At The Start Of My Real Estate Sales Career

What I thought real estate was about before I got my license and what I learned it is all about over time are vastly different. Knowing these 24 things would have been helpful.

1. **Job #1 and the most important skill to be mastered for a real estate agent is the practice of developing new relationships with people interested in buying and selling real estate** – You can be great at showing houses, negotiating, etc., but if you don't have clients to do these things for those skills are worthless.

2. **Your income will rise and fall in direct proportion to your investment of time, money and effort in prospecting** – It's a fact.

4. **Real estate sales is a contact sport** – That is not to say you must hit others, but you will get knocked around. It is not for the feint of heart.

5. **You will experience greater success if you work from a sensible business plan consisting of meaningful goals, effective systems, and a system for staying on track** – To learn more, see my book *'Planning For Success In Real Estate Sales – Your Guide To Creating A Winning Business Plan'*.

6. **Real estate sales is not always fair** – Sometimes the less deserving agent gets the listing. Sometimes you do everything right but still come out empty handed. Real estate is like life.

7. **You are never going to win them all so don't be disappointed when you lose** – That's not to say you shouldn't

learn from your failures. Just don't dwell on the ones you don't get.

8. **Never assume a listing is guaranteed yours** – Treat every listing presentation as though you were competing with three other top agents.

9. **Never burn a bridge with a colleague** – Nothing good will come of it. You may have to work with that agent again on another deal.

10. **If you're going to lose a buyer eventually, it is better to lose them quickly** – Qualify your buyers to ensure you should be working with them in the first place.

11. **It <u>does</u> take money to make money** – Real estate sales is a business. Succeeding in business requires effective utilization of time, energy, and MONEY. There is no other way around it.

12. **People don't always make the right decisions for themselves.** Just look at all the people that smoke, drink to excess, and drive without wearing a seatbelt. That's why you must learn sales techniques. Professional selling is helping people make the right choice.

13. **Ultimately, real estate agents do not sell houses; real estate agents help solve problems.** Helping sell or buy a house is just a part of a bigger picture.

14. **Some other major event is going on in your client's life at the same time they are selling or buying a home**. Understand what that is and you'll be better able to serve them. It may be a job loss (or promotion), health issue, or a child moving out (or back in). It may be another problem your client has and may not have told you. But it is certain that more is going on than just buying or selling a house.

15. **In this business you are never as rich as you feel or as poor as you feel** – Sometimes you are flush with cash, other

times you are broke. Neither situation paints a true picture of the strength (or weakness) of your business. Your systems, dedication, and effort are the true measures. So don't get depressed when your bank account is low and don't stop working when it is high.

16. **The key to success in real estate sales is 'leverage'.** Taking one opportunity and using it to create more opportunities is the key to growing your business.

17. **Control everything you can** – There are so many things beyond the control of the agent, the agent must control everything she can.

18. **Your clients are not looking for a new best friend** – They are looking for a real estate professional to help them sell or buy a house. It's good to be friendly but too many agents make the mistake of making being friends the primary goal instead of providing professional service.

19. **It's not a sale until title passes** – Or as my dear friend (and former car salesman) Doug Crawford used to say "It's not a sale until you see the taillights drive down the road."

20. **Don't count your commissions before they are earned** – And they are earned when the title passes (see #19 above).

21. **God gave you two ears and one mouth and you should use them in that proportion** – Listen twice as much as you talk.

22. **Never put a period where God has placed a comma** – You may think a deal is dead but it may not be. Never lose hope. Sometimes it is the agent's hope that is the only thing that keeps a deal alive.

23. **The broker you work under has more influence over your business than you think** – Hopefully that influence is good . . . but it may not be. That's why you should always listen to what other brokers have to say.

24. **Dollar for dollar the best investment a real estate agent can make is in a good contact management system** - Be aware however that that system is worthless without the discipline to use it.

62

59 Lessons Learned in the Trenches

It's an exaggeration to say I learned something new every day, but there have been things I learned 'on the job'. Some lessons cost me nothing but time and maybe some embarrassment. Others . . . well, I'd rather not think what they cost. Perhaps you can learn what I did without the cost through these 59 lessons.

1. Even if you put a big note next to a red button that says "DO NOT PRESS THIS BUTTON" somebody will press the button - Put a piece of tape over buttons you don't want pressed (and locks you don't want locked).

2. Before you turn on the whole house fan be sure to close the damper in the fireplace - I learned this one just before the start of an open house. It took 45 minutes for all the ash to settle before I could begin to clean it up.

3. When a buyer tells you, in response to the question of whether they are preapproved for a mortgage, "Oh, don't worry, money will not be a problem", be assured that money will indeed be a problem – And if a buyer refuses to get pre-qualified it's your own fault if you spend time on them and later learn they are not financeable.

4. Sometimes deals that come together the easiest are the hardest to get to settlement - I once put a lawn sign in front of a new listing and by the time I got back to my office I had a phone call from someone who wanted to buy that house. She made a deal and the whole thing took just a couple hours. That was the easy part. Getting her to the closing table was more difficult than with any other buyer I have worked with.

5. There are going to be deals that are so easy that at settlement you feel like a bank robber, not deserving your large fee - And you probably <u>don't</u> deserve what you get paid for that deal. But remember this: there were many deals that you worked hard on that did not come together and you were paid nothing. You did not deserve that either.

6. When a buyer you just met tells you they have been looking for a house for three years, take that as a warning – They may be 'serial lookers' or 'recreational buyers'.

7. Full-time agents that get a part-time job ('just for a while until real estate picks up') have taken the first step towards leaving the real estate sales business – It is rare when one comes back.

8. If you think open houses are a waste of time, you are right. If you think they are a great source of new client relationships, you are also right - Your attitude going into an open house is the key to whether or not it will be successful.

9. Never judge another agent based on what others have told you - Rely on your own experiences just as you would want others to do for you.

10. The day you don't shave or wear old jeans is the day a buyer walks into your office unannounced and says they want to see your new listing – Never be caught unprepared.

11. If you are going to lose, lose with your best shot - Leave nothing that could be done, undone.

12. The job of a buyer agent is to help the client get the house, not get the house at the lowest possible price - Far too often agents, in an attempt to make the deal a little better for the buyer (even though the buyer was willing to pay the seller's price), find themselves and their clients on the outside looking in when a new buyer swoops in with a higher price.

13. Never come to work with socks that have holes in them - You may have to show a house that day that requires you to remove your shoes.

14. If someone offers you money, take it - Even if you think the money is offered to you by mistake. You can always give it back if it was a mistake but you may not be able to get it again if you pass on it the first time.

15. If you have 60 minutes to do a listing presentation, spend at least 30 minutes thoroughly understanding the seller's needs by asking questions – Sellers like agents who are interested in them.

16. As a general rule, real estate agents talk too much – Speak when you have something to say, not to hear the sound of your own voice.

17. You will make more money and experience less stress if you work from a well thought out business plan – A great resource is my book, *"Planning For Success in Real Estate Sales – Your Guide to Creating a Winning Business Plan"*.

18. A real estate office is led by the strongest personality in the office – That should be the broker/manager but it may not be.

19. If being liked is important to you, do not pursue a career in real estate management – Being liked and working in management are not mutually exclusive, but you always have someone mad at you when you are the person in charge.

20. Most agents would rather go to the dentist than call a FSBO – Which is why most agents make very little money. The difference between successful agents and unsuccessful agents is successful agents make a habit of doing the things other agents will not do.

21. The key to consistent income is consistent prospecting – Consistency. Consistency. Consistency. Let me say it again. Consistency. Get the point?

**22. Technology will not replace real estate agents but real estate agents using the latest technology will replace the real

estate agents who do not – Technology has made agents far more efficient. Efficient agents can reach far more prospects creating far more opportunities.

23. There is no such thing as a nosy neighbor wasting your time at an open house - Any time you have the chance to meet a homeowner, spend time with them, and give them your card is time well spent.

24. In real estate sales you are never as rich as you feel nor are you as poor as you feel – Your wealth in in your habits, not your bank account. There have been many agents who stumbled into a huge commission check (and felt rich) but who were out of the business six months later because they had poor work habits.

25. It is always a good idea to wear slip on shoes when you show houses - Many homeowners want you to take your shoes off.

26. A client's 'no' on Monday could be a 'yes' on Wednesday - They were not lying when they said 'no', their situation may have changed or they just changed their mind. What they say is not etched in stone so don't act like it is.

27. Never pick a fight with an appraiser or building inspector – You'll never win.

28. Always lower expectations – It is better to under-promise and over-deliver than the other way around. The same outcome will be perceived differently depending on expectations.

29. Insist on all offers in writing – You want to be certain you have the terms right of course, but you also want to flesh out an insincere buyer who may just be throwing out an offer to see what the seller's response will be. Having them sign something – even if it has no legal standing – will also protect your standing with your seller client should the buyer back out of the deal. Getting an offer, thinking the house is sold, and then having the buyer back out is upsetting to any seller. They'll often turn on you for letting them get that far without having anything in writing.

31. Verify the pre-approval – A simple call to the loan officer just to verify the pre-approval you have been given is authentic. You should also ask if, "there are any red flags" that might be problematic.

32. Own your domain name – If you haven't done so by now it may be too late, but if you can, lock up the domain name www.YourName.com. It's great for branding, easy for clients to remember, and the mark of a professional. You may even be able to sell it. (I once had an agent with the same name as an adult film star. The porn actress wanted my agent's domain name and paid her several hundred dollars to release it to her.)

33. Be the resource, not the source – Unless you are rock solid certain of some fact, it is wiser for you to direct the questioner to where they can get the answer than to provide the answer yourself. You may have been given bad information. If you provide bad information, even innocently, you may be responsible for the consequences of the client acting on that information.

34. Understand the difference between a great house and a great listing – A great house is a showcase, well built, comfortable, beautiful, etc. A great listing is a house that will sell. They are not always the same thing.

35. Know where your business comes from – By knowing how your clients found you, not only will you know what lead generation systems are working for you, but it will also reveal what other systems you may not be using effectively.

36. Respond to Internet leads in seconds, not minutes – Internet searchers don't want to talk to you . . . until they do and then they want to talk to you NOW. If you're not available they go on until they find someone who is. By the time you get back to them, it's too late.

37. Use practiced scripts – For every situation there are tried and true dialogs that effectively convey your message. Learn what to say and when to say it. Practice it until it no longer sounds scripted. Not only will you be a more effective communicator, you will be able to focus on what your client is saying because you won't be distracted wondering what you should say next.

38. Send a thank you letter to the owner of the house who did not select you to be their agent – A graceful response thanking them for the interview and wishing them well may pay dividends if the agent they selected doesn't get the job done and the listing expires.

39. Always use a good pen – Give your clients reason to believe they are working with a professional – give them a quality pen to sign the listing papers or offer sheet. Use a pen with a cap. Hold onto the cap while they are using the pen and you'll never walk off without reclaiming your pen.

40. Take a lesson from Amazon on pricing – Amazon knows a thing or two about marketing. Note how they price their items – they never end in '000'. $99.99, not $100. Who knows why they do it but there must be a good reason. You should follow their example.

41. Do you have to remove a lawn sign frozen in the ground? – Take along a Thermos of hot water. Pour it over the part of the sign stuck in the ground. In a minute or so you'll be able to slide the sign out easily. This also works for putting a sign into frozen ground but you'll probably need more water.

42. Time kills all deals – Once a deal is agreed to, little good comes from moving slowly.

43. Always use visuals – Never simply tell people what you can show them. They'll remember the message longer.

44. Write your own raving fan letters - Many people would be happy to write you a letter of praise but they may not have the time or writing skills to write such a letter. Make it easy for them and write the letter for them. All they have to do is sign it.

45. If you want to sell more homes, spend more time with agents who are doing the level of business you aspire to – Associate with agents that sell a lot and you will raise your game closer to their level. Hang around low producing agents and your production will be lower.

46. If a homeowner offers you a cup of coffee, take it – They are inviting you to spend time with them. That is always good.

47. Never unsubscribe from another agent's emails – Most email blasts will have no use for you but if one does – a price reduction or back on market notice, for example – it may be worth thousands. Besides, you should always know what your competition is doing.

48. Don't expect loyalty from your clients – Loyalty is good but the client has no obligation to be loyal to the agent. Many will throw you aside if it helps them. Don't be surprised when this happens to you.

49. If it is worth doing it is worth measuring - Keep track of how many postcards you mail and how many leads they generate. The same with the money you spend on leads.

50. Never try to get between your client and their attorney – You'll lose every time.

51. Listing opportunities are everywhere – I once got a listing on the checkout line at the grocery store because I was wearing a name badge. Always be thinking 'listings' and more listing opportunities will be apparent to you.

52. Generally it is not a good idea to call clients after 8 PM - They are probably tired. They may be drunk. Either way it is not wise to conduct business when they are that way.

53. Never pretend you know something you don't – You may think you can bluff your way through but the client knows you're lying.

54. Try new things – They may not work. Then again, they might. And don't pull the plug on a new idea or system too soon. Better to pull the plug a month late than a day early.

55. Don't take rejection personally – Your prospective clients hardly know you, why would you give their decision to use another agent the power to make you feel badly about yourself? Be disappointed an opportunity was lost but let it end there.

56. Never "pour gas on a fire" – Don't elevate an already emotional situation by losing your temper, being a wise guy, provoking the other side or acting immature. Somebody has to be the adult; it should be the professional real estate agent.

57. You will do better to set the standard for your clients of being 'satisfied' rather than being 'happy' - Happy is a feeling; satisfied is a decision. The client can be satisfied (the deal surpasses their minimal standard) without bring happy (they would have liked more). Don't let them blow a satisfactory deal in order to be 'happy'.

58. It is generally not a good idea to open the refrigerator door in an abandoned house – I still get nauseous thinking about the day I learned this.

59. You would think working for a family member would be easy, but it is not – In fact, members of your family may be the most difficult clients you will ever work with.

63

7 Things I Wish I Had Done Differently Early In My Career

I spent the first eight years of my real estate career working in a small independent office with no training and little direction. I didn't know what I didn't know. If I could do it over again there are some things I would definitely do differently.

1. **Surround myself with higher producing agents earlier** - Your level of production will rise or fall proportionate with that of the average of the agents you associate with. I learned that when I joined a high producing office and saw my production increase more than 50% in the first year.

2. **Set bigger goals** – I would have sold more houses if I had aimed higher. What we think we can accomplish is a fraction of what we are capable of.

3. **Utilized a real estate business plan earlier** - It wasn't until I had been a salesperson for more than 10 years that I discovered the usefulness of an effective business plan. (For more information about real estate business plans, my book, *"Planning For Success in Real Estate Sales - Your Guide to Creating a Winning Business Plan"* is a great resource. You can find it at Amazon.com, Audible.com, and iTunes.)

4. **Branded myself** – The truth is the client buys you, not your company. I was overshadowed by my company's brand even though I was doing all the work.

5. **Joined a 95% commission company sooner** – For the first 8 years of my career I gave $1 out of every $2 I earned over to my broker. That's crazy. Today I wouldn't give 20% to the broker. I'm the one doing the work. I'm the one making the investment. The broker does provide some services and

deserves to be compensated but anything more than 20 cents on the dollar is too much.

6. **Kept better track of prospects and leads** – When I consider the number of prospects I talked to over the years – and never spoke to again because I didn't keep good records - it is staggering. If I had a system back then that captured each prospect's information, I would have sold many more houses.

7. **Enlisted the help of a coach** – All the things on this list I learned through experience, some of it painful, much of it costly. A good coach could have taught me these things – and much more – in a fraction of the time and at a fraction of the cost.

About the Author

Matt Williams has been a real estate agent, manager, coach, and broker for more than 30 years. He is owner and broker of Realty Executives – Williams-Sykes Realty located in the Hudson Valley region of New York.

Also by Matt Williams

Planning For Success in Real Estate Sales – Your Guide to Creating a Winning Business Plan

Available at Amazon.com in print and ebook format and Audible.com and iTunes in audiobook format.

For information about 1-on-1 coaching, please send an inquiry to
realexec@mac.com

www.ingramcontent.com/pod-product-compliance
Lightning Source LLC
Chambersburg PA
CBHW051652170526
45167CB00001B/434